Crochet with Leftover Yarn

Crochet WITH Leftover Yarn

Quick and easy stashbuster patterns using one ball or less

Nicki Trench

CICO BOOKS

This edition published in 2026 by CICO Books
An imprint of Ryland Peters & Small Ltd
20–21 Jockey's Fields, London WC1R 4BW
www.rylandpeters.com
Email: euregulations@rylandpeters.com

First published in 2019 as *Crochet Stashbusters*

10 9 8 7 6 5 4 3 2 1

Text © Nicki Trench 2019, 2026
Design, illustration and photography © CICO Books 2019, 2026

The designs in this book are copyright and must not be crocheted for sale.

Patterns in this book have previously appeared in one of the following titles by Nicki Trench: *Cute and Easy Crochet, Cute and Easy Crochet with Flowers, Cute and Easy Crocheted Cosies* or *Super-Cute Crochet.*

The author's moral rights have been asserted. All rights reserved. No part of this publication may be reproduced, stored in a retrieval system or transmitted in any form or by any means, electronic, mechanical, photocopying or otherwise, without the prior permission of the publisher.

A CIP record for this book is available from the British Library.

ISBN: 978-1-80065-583-6

Printed in China

Editor: Marie Clayton
Photographers: Caroline Arber, Gavin Kingcome, Emma Mitchell and Penny Wincer
Stylists: Alison Davidson, Rose Hammick, Nel Haynes, Sophie Martell and Luis Peral-Aranda
Illustrator: Stephen Dew

In-house designer: Eliana Holder
Art director: Sally Powell
Creative director: Leslie Harrington
Head of production: Patricia Harrington
Publishing manager: Penny Craig
Publisher: Cindy Richards

The authorised representative in the EEA is Authorised Rep Compliance Ltd., Ground Floor. 71 Lower Baggot Street, Dublin, D01 P593, Ireland
www.arccompliance.com

Safety note: If you are making a project for a young child, substitute the safety eyes with embroidery in yarn.

Contents

Introduction 6

CHAPTER 1
For the Home 8

Bunny Egg Cosies 10
Mug Cosies 12
Bobble Cafetière Cosy 14
Round Stripy Cushion Cover 17
Placemats 20
Vintage-style Vase Coaster 23

CHAPTER 2
For Baby 26

Beanie Hat 28
Lilac Bootees 30
Star Stitch Bootees 33
Baby Pompom Hat 36
Nursery Coat Hangers 38
Ophelia Buggy Blanket 42

CHAPTER 3
Bits and Bobs 44

Striped Phone Cosy 46
Jam Jar Tea Light Cosies 48
Bunting 51
Pin Cushions 54
Crochet Hook Cosy 57
Flower Brooch 58
Butterfly and Blossom Key Ring 60

CHAPTER 4
Toys 62

Pickle the Puppy 64
Melody the Kitten 67
Sparkles the Snowman 70
Billy the Bear 73
Sugar Mice 76
Baby Bouncers 78

Techniques 80
Template 94
Suppliers 95
Index 96

Introduction

Nowadays everyone is becoming much more aware of reusing, recycling and not throwing away as much. If that sounds like you then this is the ideal crochet book to inspire you and give you ideas of what to make to use up the yarn you already have. And what crochet lover doesn't have baskets or even boxes of leftover yarns all over their home? Sometimes a pattern only calls for less than a quarter or half of a ball of a particular colour, or you may have quite a lot of one ball left over from a project and it's super hard to throw out yarn that you have spent hours sourcing. We all know yarn is not cheap; also… well sometimes the texture just feels so good. Throwing out leftover yarn is like throwing out a half-eaten bar of chocolate, and who does that!

This collection has been put together with leftover yarns in mind, using a fantastic collection of my patterns from different books. There are 25 designs, featuring projects for the home, including one of my favourite cushion covers, a cafetière cosy to keep fresh coffee warm; and projects for babies – cute hats, bootees and even a blanket using many different colours. The Toys section has really cute amigurumi toys and a pattern for one of my granddaughter's favourite stripy bears. There is also a Bits and Bobs section which has a mix of simply delightful little makes. I absolutely love the jam jar tea light cosies and the bunting is so sweet for a child's room or to hang in the garden for summer parties.

Don't be worried about your skill level. Most of the projects in the book are simple, and in case you're not quite sure what an abbreviation means, or how to do a particular stitch, lots of the techniques are also explained at the back of the book.

Of course you don't have to use the exact colours or yarns that are given in this book – these are there as a guide. Be creative and mix and match the colours that are sitting in your own stash. If you want to substitute another yarn, tension is given where essential, and you can try different hook sizes to achieve the same measurements with a different yarn. The weight, length per ball and material blend of the yarn are also given to help you find a match from what you already have. In many cases, exact tension and even finished size are not overly important, so feel free to experiment.

If you're at a loose end and you have the urge to feed your crochet addiction, there's no need to waste time searching on the internet or your yarn shops to buy new yarn, just get rummaging in your boxes, pick up your hook and off you go.

CHAPTER 1
For the Home

Bunny Egg Cosies

These cute little egg cosies have bunny ears and are made using standard double crochet to fit an average-sized egg. They are made in a spiral so it's useful to use a stitch marker to mark the beginning and end of each round.

YARN AND MATERIALS

You can use any DK (light worsted) 100% wool yarn for these little cosies

1 part ball each of:
- Green (A)
- Blue (B)
- Deep pink (C)
- Yellow (D)

4 small pink beaded fabric bows

HOOKS AND EQUIPMENT

3.5mm (US size E/4) crochet hook

Stitch marker

Yarn needle

TENSION

17 sts x 19 rows over a 10cm (4in) square, working double crochet using 3.5mm (US size E/4) hook.

FINISHED MEASUREMENTS

Approx. 4cm (1½in) diameter

ABBREVIATIONS

approx.	approximate(ly)
ch	chain
cont	continu(e)ing
dc	double crochet
dc2tog	double crochet 2 stitches together
rep	repeat
RS	right side
ss	slip stitch
st(s)	stitch(es)
WS	wrong side

Cosy

(make 1 each in A, B, C, and D)

Make 2ch, 6dc into second ch from hook.

Round 1 (RS): 2dc in each dc to end. (*12 dc*)

Cont in rounds with RS always facing.

Round 2: Rep Round 1. (*24 dc*)

Rounds 3–7: 1dc in each dc to end.

Round 8: *1dc in next dc, dc2tog over next 2 dc; rep from * to end. (*16 dc*)

Round 9: 1dc in each dc, join with a ss in first dc of round. Fasten off.

Ears

(make 2 per Cosy)

Row 1: Using A, B, C, or D, make 5ch, 1dc in second ch from hook, 1dc in each ch to end. (*4 sts*)

Rows 2–5: 1ch, 1dc in each st to end. (*4 sts*)

Row 6: 1ch, [dc2tog] twice. (*2 sts*)

Row 7: 1ch, 1dc in each st.

Row 8: 1ch, dc2tog.

Fasten off.

Finishing

Sew in ends on WS and turn Cosy RS out.

Pin and block Ears.

Position and pin Ears onto top of RS of Cosy and sew in place.

Sew one bow onto the left-hand Ear.

YARN AND MATERIALS

Debbie Bliss Rialto DK (100% merino wool; approx. 105m/115yd per 50g/1¾oz ball) DK (light worsted) weight yarn
 1 part ball for each cosy of shades:
 57 Banana (yellow)
 82 Mallard (blue-green)

1 button per cosy

HOOKS AND EQUIPMENT

3.5mm (US size E/4) crochet hook

Yarn needle

Sewing needle and thread to match button

TENSION

17 sts x 19 rows over a 10cm (4in) square, working double crochet using 3.5mm (US size E/4) hook and Debbie Bliss Rialto DK.

FINISHED MEASUREMENTS

26 x 7.5cm (10¼ x 3in), to fit an average sized mug

NOTE

The multiple is 14 sts + 1 st (+ 1 for the base ch).

ABBREVIATIONS

approx.	approximate(ly)
ch	chain
dc	double crochet
rep	repeat
RS	right side
ss	slip stitch
st(s)	stitch(es)
tr	treble

Mug Cosies

These make a very cute present, and they're also great for keeping your own cup of tea or coffee nice and warm.

Cosy

Row 1: Make 16ch, 1dc in second ch from hook, 1dc in each ch to end. (*15 sts*)
Row 2 (RS): 3ch, 3tr in first st, *miss 3 sts, 1dc in each of next 7 sts, miss 3 sts, 4tr in last st.
Row 3: 1ch, 1dc in each st to end, 1dc in top of 3-ch from previous row. (*15 sts*)
Row 4: 1ch, 1dc in each of first 4 sts, miss 3 sts, 7tr in next st, miss 3 sts, 1dc in last 4 sts.
Row 5: 1ch, 1dc in each st to end. (*15 sts*)
Row 6: 3ch, 3tr in first st, miss 3 sts, 1dc in each of next 7 sts, miss 3 sts, 4tr in last st.
Rep Rows 2–6 five more times.
Rep Rows 2–5 once more.

TAB
Row 1: Ss in each of next 4 sts, 1dc in each of next 7 sts, ss in each of next 4 sts.
Fasten off.
Row 2: With RS facing, rejoin yarn in first dc from previous Row. 1ch, 1dc in same st, 1dc in each of next 6 sts, turn. (*7 sts*)
Row 3: 1ch, 1dc in first st, 1dc in each of next 6 sts. (*7 sts*)
Row 4: Rep Row 3.
Row 5 (buttonhole): 1ch, 1dc in each of next 2 sts, miss 3 ch, 1dc in last 2 sts.
Row 6: 1ch, 1dc in each of next 2 sts, 3dc in ch sp, 1dc in each of last 2 sts.
Fasten off.

Finishing

Sew in ends.

Sew on button on other side of Cosy to align with buttonhole.

Bobble Cafetière Cosy

The bobble stitch used for this cosy creates a lovely thick fabric, which will keep your coffee piping hot. If you have lots of small scraps of yarn, you can make every band a different colour.

YARN AND MATERIALS

King Cole Merino Blend DK (100% wool; approx. 104m/114yd per 50g/1¾oz ball) DK (light worsted) weight yarn

1 ball each of shades:
- 3090 Carnation (pale pink) (A)
- 3088 Bayleaf (dark green) (B)
- 855 Mustard (yellow) (C)
- 1531 Pale Blue (D)
- 907 Raspberry (dark pink) (E)
- 853 Sage (pale green) (F)
- 3294 Plum (purple) (G)

HOOKS AND EQUIPMENT

4mm (US size G/6) crochet hook

Yarn needle

1 large wooden button

2 small wooden buttons

TENSION

Approx. 4 bobbles across x 10 bobble rows over a 10cm (4in) square, using 4mm (US size G/6) hook and King Cole Merino Blend DK yarn.

FINISHED MEASUREMENTS

Approx. 30 x 17.5cm (12 x 7in), to fit a medium-size 4–6 cup cafetière, approx. 30cm (12in) circumference

NOTE

The multiple is 4 sts + 3 sts (+ 1 for the base ch).

ABBREVIATIONS

approx.	approximate(ly)
ch	chain
cont	continu(e)ing
dc	double crochet
dc2tog	double crochet 2 stitches together
rep	repeat
RS	right side
ss	slip stitch
st(s)	stitch(es)
tr	treble
WS	wrong side
yrh	yarn round hook

SPECIAL ABBREVIATION

5trCL (5 treble cluster/bobble): yrh, insert hook in st, yrh, pull yarn through work (3 loops on hook). Yrh, pull yarn through first 2 loops on hook (2 loops on hook). Yrh, insert hook in same st, yrh, pull yarn through work (4 loops on hook), yrh, pull yarn through first 2 loops on hook (3 loops left on hook). Yrh, insert hook in same st, yrh, pull yarn through work (5 loops on hook), yrh, pull yarn through first 2 loops on hook (4 loops left on hook). Yrh, insert hook in same st, yrh, pull yarn through work (6 loops on hook), yrh, pull yarn through first 2 loops on hook (5 loops left on hook). Yrh, insert hook in same st, yrh, pull yarn through work (7 loops on hook), yrh, pull yarn through first 2 loops on hook (6 loops left on hook). Yrh, pull yarn through all 6 loops on hook (1 loop left on hook). Make 1ch to complete 5trCL.

Cosy

Work from top to bottom of Cosy.
Using A, make 44ch.
Row 1 (RS): 1dc in second ch from hook, 1dc in each ch to end. (*43 sts*)
Begin bobble pattern:
Row 2 (WS): 1ch, *1dc in each of next 3 sts, 5trCL in next st; rep from * to last 3 sts, 1dc in each of last 3 sts. (*10 bobbles*).
Cut yarn, do not fasten off.
Row 3: Join B, 1ch, *1dc in each of next 3 sts, 1dc in top of next 5trCL; rep from * to last 3 sts, 1dc in each of last 3 sts.
Row 4: 1ch, 1dc in first st, 5trCL in next st, *1dc in each of next 3 sts, 5trCL in next st; rep from * to last st, 1dc in last st. (*11 bobbles*)
Cut yarn, do not fasten off.
Row 5: Join C, 1ch, 1dc in first st, *1dc in top of next 5trCL, 1dc in each of next 3 sts; rep from * to last 5trCL, 1dc in top of last 5trCL, 1dc in last st.
Rep Rows 2–5, using A, B, C, D, E, F and G to change colour every two Rows until 16 bobble rows have been worked ending on a Row 5.
Fasten off.

Tip

When working a double crochet into the top of the 5-treble cluster, make the double crochet stitch into the chain at the top of the cluster.

Tab
Using A, make 13ch.
Row 1: 1dc in 8th ch from hook, 1dc in each of next 5 ch.
Row 2: 1ch, 1dc in each of next 6 dc, 1dc in each of next 3 ch, 2dc in next ch, 1dc in each of next 9 ch (working on underside of these 9 ch).
Row 3: 1ch, 1dc in each of next 9 dc, 2dc in each of next 2 dc, 1dc in each of next 8 dc, ss in last dc.
Fasten off.

Finishing
With RS together join top of side seams for approx. 2.5cm (1in) leaving remaining seam open.

Turn RS out.

With RS together, sew Tab to bottom of side edge, approx. 1cm (⅜in) from corner.

Sew large button on bottom of Cosy to correspond with buttonhole on Tab.

Sew small buttons on edging: Button 1 between second and third bobble from bottom and Button 2 between second and third bobble from top, on same side as large button.

SMALL BUTTON LOOPS
With RS facing, and using A, join yarn to align with side of Button 1, in dc of edging on same side as Tab. 1ch, 1dc in same st, 3ch, miss 1 st, 1dc in next st. Fasten off.

Repeat for Button 2. Fasten off.

Sew in ends.

EDGING
With RS facing, join A in top left-hand corner (of Row 1).
Row 1:
Side 1
1ch, [1dc in each of next 5 rows down first side edge, dc2tog over next 2 rows] 4 times, 1dc in each row to corner (second corner), [1dc, 1ch, 1dc] in corner st.
Bottom edge
*1dc in top of 5trCL, 1dc in each of next 3 sts; rep from * to next corner. [1dc, 1ch, 1dc] in corner st.
Side 2
[1dc in each of next 5 rows down first side edge, dc2tog over next 2 rows] 4 times, 1dc in each row to corner (third corner), [1dc, 1ch, 1dc] in corner st.
Top edge
*1dc in each of next 3 sts, 1dc in top of 5trCL; rep from * to next corner, [1dc, 1ch, 1dc] in corner st, join with a ss in first dc.
Row 2: 1ch, work a dc edge by working 1dc in each st and 3dc in each corner ch sp, join with a ss in first dc.
Fasten off.

Round Stripy Cushion Cover

Crochet is perfect for making circles and this cushion cover is a project I've been teaching to all my beginner students for many years, because it is beautiful and easy to make. It uses simple treble stitch and Aran (worsted) weight yarn.

YARN AND MATERIALS

Rowan Handknit Cotton (100% cotton; 85m/93yd per 50g/1¾oz ball) Aran (worsted) weight yarn
 1 ball each of shades:
 345 Cloud (pale blue) (A)
 353 Violet (purple) (B)
 303 Sugar (pink) (C)
 370 Forest (grey-green) (D)
 356 Raspberry (red) (E)
 309 Celery (pale green) (F)
40cm (16in) round cushion pad

HOOKS AND EQUIPMENT

5mm (US size H/8) crochet hook

Yarn needle

TENSION

14tr x 8 rows over a 10cm (4in) square, using 5mm (US size H/8) hook and Rowan Handknit Cotton.

FINISHED MEASUREMENTS

To fit a 40cm (16in) diameter circular cushion pad

ABBREVIATIONS

ch	chain
cont	continue
dc	double crochet
ss	slip stitch
tr	treble
WS	wrong side

Cushion cover

(make 2 sides)

Using A, make 6ch, join with ss in first ch.
Round 1: 3ch (counts as first tr), 11tr in circle, join with a ss in top of first 3-ch.
Change to B.
Round 2: 3ch, 1tr in same st, 2tr in each st to end of round, join with a ss in top of first 3-ch. (*24 sts*)
Change to C.
Round 3: 3ch, 1tr in same st, *1tr in next st, 2tr in each of next 2 sts; rep from * to last 2 sts, 1tr in next st, 2tr in last st, join with a ss in top of first 3-ch. (*40 sts*)
Change to D.

Round 4: 3ch, 1tr in same st, *1tr in each of next 3 sts, 2tr in next st; rep from * to last 3 sts, 1tr in each of last 3 sts, join with a ss in top of first 3-ch. (*50 sts*)
Change to E.
Round 5: 3ch, 1tr in same st, *1tr in each of next 4 sts, 2tr in next st; rep from * to last 4 sts, 1tr in each of last 4 sts, join with ss in top of first 3-ch. (*60 sts*)
Change to F.
Round 6: 3ch, 1tr in same st, *1tr in each of next 5 sts, 2tr in next st; rep from *to last 5 sts, 1tr in each of last 5 sts, join with a ss in top of first 3-ch. (*70 sts*)
Change to A.
Round 7: 3ch, 1tr in same st, *1tr in each of next 6 sts, 2tr in next st; rep from * to last 6 sts, 1tr in each of last 6 sts, join with a ss in top of first 3-ch. (*80 sts*)
Change to B.
Round 8: 3ch, 1tr in same st, *1tr in each of next 7 sts, 2tr in next st; rep from *to last 7 sts, 1tr in each of last 7 sts, join with a ss in top of first 3-ch. (*90 sts*)
Change to C.
Round 9: 3ch, 1tr in same st, *1tr in each of next 8 sts, 2tr in next st; rep from * to last 8 sts, 1tr in each of last 8 sts, join with a ss in top of first 3-ch. (*100 sts*)
Change to D.
Round 10: As Round 5. (*120 sts*)
Change to E.
Round 11: 3ch, 1tr in same st, *1tr in each of next 11 tr, 2tr in next st; rep from * to last 11 tr, 1tr in each of last 11 tr, join with a ss in top of first 3-ch. (*130 sts*)
Change to F.

Round 12: 3ch, 1tr in same st, *1tr in each of next 12 tr, 2tr in next st; rep from * to last 12 tr, 1tr in last 12 tr, join with a ss in top of first 3-ch. (*140 sts*)
Change to A.
Round 13: As Round 7. (*160 sts*)
Change to B.
Round 14: 3ch, 1tr in same st, *1tr in each of next 15 tr, 2tr in next st, rep from * to last 15 tr, 1tr in each of last 15 tr, join with a ss in top of first 3-ch. (*170 sts*)
Change to C.
Round 15: 3ch, 1tr in same st, *1tr in each of next 16 tr, 2tr in next st; rep from * to last 16 tr, 1tr in each of last 16 tr, join with a ss in top of first 3-ch. (*180 sts*)
Change to D.
Round 16: As Round 9. (*200 sts*)

Finishing

Put cushion sides WS facing. Insert hook into both sides and, using A, make 1ch. Make 1dc in each st, putting hook through both sides and joining sides together, leaving a big enough gap to push through cushion pad. Cont in dc until seam is fully joined together.

Fasten off. Sew in ends.

Placemats

Here I've used a yarn that is a recycled jersey cotton, but you can also make these placemats by cutting up strips of fabric – it's a great opportunity to use up old t-shirts! And if you don't have enough yarn left for a placemat, just crochet fewer rounds to make a coaster with a single flower in the centre, or a teapot stand with fewer flowers around the edge.

YARN AND MATERIALS

Mats
Hoooked Zpagetti (92% recycled cotton/ 8% other recycled fibres; approx. 120m/131yd per 850g/30oz ball) super chunky (super bulky) weight yarn
   1 ball each of shades:
   Pink (A)
   Pink red (B)
   Fuchsia (C)
   White (D)

Flowers
You can use any 100% cotton DK (light worsted) or 4-ply (fingering) yarn for these
   1 part ball each of shades:
   Blue (E)
   Deep pink (F)
   Yellow (G)
   White (H)
   Leaf green (J)
   Coral (K)

HOOKS AND EQUIPMENT

3.5mm (US size E/4) and 9mm (US size M/13) crochet hooks

Sewing needle and thread to match each petal colour

TENSION

7 sts x 7 rows over a 10cm (4in) square working double crochet using 9mm (US size M/13) hook and Hoooked Zpagetti

FINISHED MEASUREMENTS

Approx. 33cm (13in) in diameter

ABBREVIATIONS

ch	chain
cont	continu(e)ing
dc	double crochet
rep	repeat
RS	right side
ss	slip stitch
st(s)	stitch(es)
tr	treble

NOTE

This is made using a fabric yarn with strands that are inconsistent in thickness. The pattern is a guide to making the mats, but if your work begins to go wavy, make one row of double crochet without increasing and then increase on the next round, which will keep the mat flat.

Mat

(make 1 in each of A, B, C and D)
Using 9mm (US size M/13) hook, make 6ch, join with a ss in first ch to form a ring.
Round 1 (RS): 1ch, 8dc in ring. (*8 sts*)
Cont in rounds with RS always facing. Mark first st of each round with a stitch marker to keep track of where round starts and ends.
Round 2: 2dc in each st. (*16 sts*)
Round 3: *2dc in next st, 1dc in next st; rep from * to end. (*24 sts*)
Round 4: 1dc in each st to end. (*24 sts*)
Round 5: *2dc in next st, 1dc in next st; rep from * to end. (*36 sts*)
Round 6: Rep Round 4. (*36 sts*)
Round 7: *2dc in next st, 1dc in each of next 2 sts; rep from * to end. (*48 sts*)
Round 8: Rep Round 4. (*48 sts*)
Round 9: *2dc in next st, 1dc in each of next 3 sts; rep from * to end. (*60 sts*)
Round 10: Rep Round 4. (*72 sts*)
Round 11: *2dc in next st, 1dc in each of next 4 sts; rep from * to end. (*72 sts*)
Fasten off.

Flower

(make 16 per mat, using any two of E, F, G, H, J and K, for each mat)
Using 3.5mm (US size E/4) hook and first colour, make 7ch, join with a ss in first ch.
Round 1 (centre): 1ch, 14dc in ring, join with a ss in first dc.
Fasten off first colour.
Round 2 (petals): Join second colour with a ss in any dc, [3ch, 2tr in next st, 3ch, 1ss in next st] 7 times, working last ss in base of first 3ch.
Fasten off.

Finishing

Sew in ends. Using matching sewing thread, sew one flower in centre of RS of each mat and 15 evenly spaced around the outside edge.

Vintage-style Vase Coaster

Vintage crochet mats are very popular at the moment, so why not make your own? Traditionally mats were made using very fine cotton yarn, but I've used DK (light worsted)-weight cotton for a much quicker project. The pattern is a little intricate, but the stitches are easy. Make sure you block and press when finished.

YARN AND MATERIALS
Rowan Cotton Glacé (100% cotton; approx 115m/125yd per 50g/1¾oz ball) DK (light worsted) weight yarn

Mat 1
1 ball each of shades:
832 Persimmon (orange) (A)
725 Ecru (off-white) (B)
867 Precious (purple) (C)
845 Shell (pale pink) (D)
814 Shoot (green) (E)

Mat 2
1 ball each of shades:
861 Rose (deep pink) (A)
845 Shell (pale pink) (B)
867 Precious (purple) (C)
725 Ecru (off-white) (D)
833 Ochre (yellow) (E)

HOOKS AND EQUIPMENT
3mm (US size D/3) crochet hook

TENSION
First 4 rounds of mat pattern measure 13.5cm (5¼in) in diameter using 3mm (US size D/3) hook and Rowan Cotton Glacé.

FINISHED MEASUREMENTS
28cm (11in) in diameter

ABBREVIATIONS
ch	chain
cont	continu(e)ing
dc	double crochet
dtr	double treble
rep	repeat
RS	right side
sp(s)	space(s)
ss	slip stitch
st(s)	stitch(es)
tr	treble

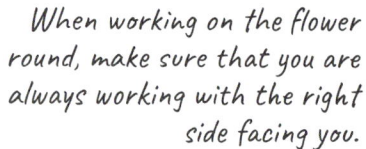

Tip

When working on the flower round, make sure that you are always working with the right side facing you.

Coaster

Using A, make 6ch, join with a ss in first ch to form a ring.
Round 1 (RS): 3ch (counts as 1tr), 2tr in ring, 2ch, [3tr, 2ch] 5 times in ring, join with a ss in top of first 3-ch.
Fasten off A.
Cont in rounds with RS always facing.
Round 2: Join B with a ss in any 2ch sp, 3ch, [2tr, 2ch, 3tr] in same 2ch sp, 1ch, *[3tr, 2ch, 3tr, 1ch] in next 2ch sp; rep from * 4 times, join with a ss in top of first 3-ch.
Fasten off B.
Round 3: Join C with a ss in any 1ch sp, 3ch (counts as 1tr), 2tr in same 1ch sp, 1ch, *[3tr, 2ch, 3tr, 1ch] in next 2ch sp, 3tr in next 1ch sp, 1ch; rep from * 4 times, [3tr, 2ch, 3tr, 1ch] in next 2ch sp, join with a ss in top of first 3-ch.
Break off C, but do not fasten off.
Round 4: Join in D, 1ss in next tr (centre st of 3tr group), 3ch (counts as 1tr), 2tr in same place as ss just worked, 1dc in next 1ch sp, 1ch, *[1tr, 1ch] 6 times in next 2ch sp, 1dc in next 1ch sp**, 3tr in centre st of next 3tr group, 1dc in next 1ch sp, 1ch; rep from * ending last rep at **, join with a ss in top of first 3-ch.
Break off D, but do not fasten off.
Round 5: Join in E, 4ch (counts as 1dtr), 1tr in top of first 3ch in previous round, 1tr in each of next 2 tr, 1dtr in next dc, *4ch, 1dc in 1ch sp in centre of next 6tr group, 4ch**, 1dtr in next dc, 1tr in each of next 3 tr, 1dtr in next dc; rep from * ending last rep at **, join with a ss in top of first 4-ch.
Do not fasten off.
Round 6: Cont with E, 3ch (counts as 1tr), *1tr in each of next 3 tr, 1tr in next dtr, 7tr in next 4ch sp, miss next dc, 7tr in next 4ch sp**, 1tr in next dtr; rep from * ending last rep at **, join with a ss in top of first 3-ch.
Break off E, but do not fasten off.
Round 7: Join in B (or D), 1ch, *miss next 2 tr, [2tr, 2ch, 2tr] in next tr, miss next 2 tr, 1dc in next tr; rep from * omitting dc at end of last rep, join with a ss in top of first tr at beg of round.
Do not fasten off.
Round 8: Cont with B (or D), 3ch (counts as 1tr), 1tr in next tr, *[2tr, 2ch, 2tr] in next 2ch sp, 1tr in each of next 2 tr**, miss next dc, 1tr in each of next 2 tr; rep from * ending last rep at **, join with a ss in top of first 3-ch.
Fasten off B (or D).
Round 9 (flower round): Join A with a ss in any 2ch sp, 1ch, 1dc in same 2ch sp, *4ch, form a ring by joining with a ss in first ch of 4ch just made, [3ch, 1tr in ring, 3ch, 1ss in ring] 5 times (5 petals – 1 flower – made), 1ss in dc at base of flower, 1dc in each of next 8 tr**, 1dc in next 2ch sp; rep from * ending last rep at **, join with a ss in first dc.
Fasten off.

Finishing

Block, starch and press.

CHAPTER 2
For Baby

Beanie Hat

This is a really simple beanie hat pattern decorated with a pretty boat motif. Always use a very soft yarn if making something that will be worn on a baby's head.

YARN AND MATERIALS

Baby yarn such as Debbie Bliss Baby Cashmerino (55% wool, 33% acrylic, 12% cashmere; approx 125m/136yd per 50g/1¾oz ball)
  1 ball of Off-white or Ecru (A)
  1 part ball each of shades:
  Pale green (B)
  Pale blue (C)
  Scraps of red, white and blue for the boat motif

HOOKS AND EQUIPMENT

3mm (US size D/3) and 2.5mm (US size C/2) crochet hooks

Yarn needle

TENSION

18 sts x 13 rows over a 10cm (4in) square working in half-treble using a 3mm (US size D/3) hook.

SIZE

To fit age: 3–6 months

FINISHED MEASUREMENTS

Circumference: 36cm (14in)

ABBREVIATIONS

approx.	approximate(ly)
ch	chain
dc	double crochet
dtr	double treble
htr	half-treble
qtr	quadruple treble
rep	repeat
ss	slip stitch
st(s)	stitch(es)
ttr	triple treble
WS	wrong side

Hat

Using A and 3mm (US size D/3) hook, make 4ch, ss in first ch to make a ring.

Round 1: 2ch, make 8htr into ring, join with ss in first 2-ch. (*8 sts*)

Round 2: 2ch, 1htr in same st, 2htr in each st to end, join with ss in first 2-ch. (*16 sts*)

Round 3: 2ch, 1htr in same st, *1htr in next st, 2htr in next st; rep from * to end, join with ss in first 2-ch. (*24 sts*)

Round 4: Rep Round 3. (*36 sts*)

Round 5: 2ch, 1htr in same st, *1htr in each of next 2 sts, 2htr in next st; rep from * to last 2 sts, 1htr in last 2 sts, join with ss in first 2-ch. (*48 sts*)

Round 6: 2ch, 1htr in same st, *1htr in each of next 7 sts, 2htr in next st; rep from * to last 7 sts, 1htr in each st to end, join with ss in first 2-ch. (*54 sts*)

Round 7: 2ch, 1htr in same st, *1htr in each of next 8 sts, 2htr in next st; rep from * to last 8 sts, 1htr in each st to end, join with ss in first 2-ch. (*60 sts*)

Rounds 8–14: 2ch, 1htr in each st to end, join with ss in first 2-ch.
Join in B.

Round 15: 1ch, 1dc in each st to end, join with ss.
Join in C.

Round 16: 1ch, 1dc in each st to end, join with ss.
Fasten off.

Boat motif base

Using red and 2.5mm (US size C/2) hook, make 9ch, 1dc in next ch from hook, 1htr in next ch, 1tr in next ch, 1dtr in next ch, 1tr in next ch, 1htr in next ch, 1dc, ss in first ch.
Fasten off.

Boat motif sails

Using white and 2.5mm (US size C/2) hook, make 11ch, make 1dc in second ch from hook, 1dc in next ch, 1htr in next ch, 1tr in each of next 2ch, 1dtr in next ch, 1ttr in next ch, 1qtr in next ch.
Fasten off.
Working on other side of ch just worked with WS facing, join blue in underside of second dc, 1dc in next ch, 1htr in next ch, 1tr in next ch, 1dtr in next ch, 1ttr in next ch 1qtr in next ch, 6ch, join with ss in next ch.
Fasten off.

Finishing

Sew boat motif sail onto boat base using yarn needle and attaching to the center bottom chain of the straighter edge of the bottom of boat.

Sew boat motif onto hat.

Lilac Bootees

These cute little slippers have a strap to keep them in place, and they are great for using up the odd ball of yarn.

YARN AND MATERIALS

Debbie Bliss Baby Cashmerino (55% wool, 33% acrylic, 12% cashmere; 125m/136yd per 50g/1¾oz ball) lightweight DK (sport) weight yarn
- 1 ball of shade 608 Pale Lilac (A)
- 1 part ball of shade 10 Lilac (B)

2 small buttons

HOOKS AND EQUIPMENT

3mm (US size D/3) crochet hook

Stitch marker

Yarn needle

TENSION

Exact tension is not essential for this project, just adjust the hook size as necessary to achieve a firm fabric.

SIZE

To fit age: newborn baby

FINISHED MEASUREMENTS

Length: approx. 9cm (3½in)

ABBREVIATIONS

ch	chain
dc	double crochet
htr	half treble
rep	repeat
sp	space
ss	slip stitch
st(s)	stitch(es)
tr	treble

Bootees

(make 2)

Using A, make 12ch.

Round 1: 1dc in second ch from hook, 1dc in each of next 9ch, 6dc in last ch.
Working on other side of chain, 1dc in each ch to last ch, 2dc in last ch, join with ss in first st.

Round 2: 1ch, 1dc in each of next 6 sts, 1htr in each of next 5 sts, *2htr in next st, 1htr in next st; rep from * once more, 2htr in next st, 1htr in each of next 5 sts, 1dc in each of next 7 sts, join with ss in first ch.

Round 3: 1ch, 1dc in next st, 2dc in next st, 1dc in each of next 4 sts, 1htr in each of next 6 sts, *2htr in next st, 1htr in next st; rep from * twice more, 2htr in next st, 1htr in each of next 6 sts, 1dc in each of next 4 sts, 2dc in next st, 1dc in next st, 2dc in last st, join with ss in first ch.

Round 4: 2ch, 2htr in next st, 1htr in each of next 16 sts, *2htr in next st, 1htr in next st; rep from * once more, 2htr in next st, 1htr in each of next 16 sts, 2htr in next st, 1htr in last st, join with ss in top of first ch.
Join in B, do not fasten off A.

Round 5: Using B, 2ch, 1htr in each st to end, join with ss in top of first ch.
Fasten off B.

Round 6: Using A, 1ch, 1dc in each st to end, ss in top of first ch, turn.

BEGIN WORKING IN ROWS.

Row 1: 1ch, miss first st, 1dc in next st, miss 1 st, 1dc in each of next 14 sts, *miss 1 st, 1dc in each of next 4 sts; rep from * twice more, miss 1 st, 1dc in each of next 14 sts, miss 1 st, join with ss in top of first ch.

Row 2: 1ch, 1dc in each of next 14 sts, *miss 1 st, 1dc in each of next 3 sts; rep from * twice more, miss 1 st, 1dc in each st to end.

30 For Baby

Tip

Reverse the colours to make a darker bootee with pale edging stitches.

Lilac Bootees **31**

Row 3: 1ch, 1dc in each of next 15 sts, *miss 1 st, 1dc in each of next 4 sts; rep from * once more, miss 1 st, 1dc in each st to end.

Place a st marker in the center front st.

LEFT-HAND SIDE

Row 1: 1ch, 1dc in each st to center point, miss center st, turn.
Row 2: 1ch, miss 1 st, 1dc in each st to end, turn.
Row 3: 1ch, 1dc in each st to last 4 sts, miss 1 st, 1dc in next st, miss 1 st, 1dc in last st, turn.
Row 4: 1ch, miss 1 st, 1dc in each st to end, turn.
Row 5: 1ch, 1dc in each st to last 2 sts, miss 1 st, 1dc in last st, turn.
Row 6: 1ch, miss 1 st, 1dc in each st to end, turn.
Row 7: 1ch, 1dc in each st to end.
Fasten off.

RIGHT-HAND SIDE

Join A to st next to center front (do not use center st).
Row 1: 1ch, 1dc in each st, join with ss to center back, turn.
Row 2: 1ch, 1dc in each st to last 4 sts, miss 1 st, 1dc, miss 1 st, 1dc, turn.
Row 3: 1ch, miss 1 st, 1dc in next st, 1dc in each st to end, turn.
Row 4: 1ch, 1dc in each st to last 2 sts, miss 1 st, 1dc in last st, turn.
Row 5: 1ch, miss 1 st, 1dc in each st to end, turn.
Rows 6–7: 1ch, 1dc in each st to end.
Fasten off.

Join B in center back st, work 1dc around edge of bootee opening including center front st.
Fasten off.

Straps (make 2)

Using A, make 11ch.
Row 1: 1dc in second ch from hook, 1dc in each st to end, turn.
Row 2: 1ch, 1dc in each st to end.
Row 3: 1ch, 1dc in each of next 7 sts, 2ch, miss 2 sts, 1dc in each st to end.
Row 4: 1ch, 1dc in each st (including 1dc in 2-ch) to end.
Fasten off.

Finishing

Sew strap on left for right bootee and on right for left bootee. Sew on buttons to match straps.

YARN AND MATERIALS

Debbie Bliss Baby Cashmerino (55% wool, 33% acrylic, 12% cashmere; 125m/136yd per 50g/1¾oz ball) lightweight DK (sport) weight yarn
  1 ball of shade 018 Citrus (green)

2 small toggle buttons

HOOKS AND EQUIPMENT

3mm (US size D/3) crochet hook

Yarn sewing needle

TENSION

Exact tension is not essential for this project, just adjust the hook size as necessary to achieve a firm fabric.

SIZE

To fit age: 0–6 months

FINISHED MEASUREMENTS

Length: approx 9cm (3½in)

ABBREVIATIONS

ch	chain
dc	double crochet
htr	half treble
patt	pattern
rep	repeat
RS	right side
ss	slip stitch
st(s)	stitch(es)
yoh	yarn over hook

SPECIAL ABBREVIATIONS

SS1 (star stitch 1): 3ch, insert hook in second ch from hook, yoh, pull yarn through (2 loops on hook), insert hook in next ch, yoh, pull yarn through (3 loops on hook), insert hook in base of ch, yoh, pull yarn through (4 loops on hook), insert hook in each of next 2 sts bringing a loop through each time (6 loops on the hook) yoh, pull yarn through all 6 loops, 1ch

SS2 (star stitch 2): insert hook through 1-ch of SS just made, pull yarn through (2 loops on hook), insert hook through front of last loop of previous SS, pull yarn through, insert hook through base st of last loop of previous SS, pull yarn through, *insert hook through next st and pull loop through; rep from * once more (6 loops on hook), yoh, pull yarn through all 6 loops, 1ch

Star Stitch Bootees

Use a pretty toggle to embellish these cute little bootees. The star stitch is simple once you get the idea and these would make a perfect gift.

Base

(make 2)
Make 14ch.

Round 1: 2dc in second ch from hook, 1dc in each of next 5ch, 1htr in each of next 5ch, 2htr in next ch, 3htr in last ch. (*17 sts*)
Working on other side of chain, 2htr in next ch, 1htr in each of next 5ch, 1dc in each of next 5 sts, 2dc in last ch, join with ss in top of first dc. (*31 sts*)

Round 2: 3ch, 2tr in base of ss, 1tr in next st, 2tr in next st. 1tr in each of next 9 sts, *3tr in next st, 1tr in next st; rep from * 3 times more, 1tr in each of next 9 sts, 2tr in next st, join with ss in top of first 3-ch. (*41 sts*)

Round 3: 3ch, 1tr in base of ss, 1tr in each of next 20 sts, 2tr in next st, 1tr in next st, 2tr in next st, 1tr in each of next 17 sts, 2tr in next st, join with ss in top of first 3-ch. (*46 sts*)

BEGIN WORKING STAR ST PATT IN ROWS

Row 1: SS1 once, [SS2] to end of row, join with ss in first 3-ch, turn.
Row 2: 2ch, 2htr in center of each star stitch to end of row, join with ss in top of first 3-ch. (*46 sts*)
Fasten off.

Top

(make 1 left and 1 right)
Make 40ch.
Row 1: SS1 once, [SS2] to end of row.
Row 2: 2ch, 2htr in center of each star stitch to end of row, join with ss in top of first 3-ch.
Row 3: SS1 once, [SS2] to end of row, join with a ss in first 2-ch.
Row 4: As Row 2. (For left foot shaping only, fasten off and see instruction above right for left foot shaping).

SHAPING FOR RIGHT FOOT
Row 1: SS1 once, [SS2] 4 times, 1htr in top of 2-ch from previous row, turn.
Row 2: 2ch, 1htr in center of first star stitch, 2htr in center of each of next 2 star stitches, 1htr in last star stitch, 1dc in top of first star stitch from previous row, turn.
Row 3: SS1 once, [SS2] 3 times, 1htr in top of 2-ch from previous row, turn.
Row 4: 2ch, 1htr in center of first star stitch, 2htr in next star stitch, 1htr into last star stitch, 1dc in top of star stitch from previous row, turn.
Row 5: SS1 once, SS2 once, 1htr in top of 2-ch from previous row, turn.
Fasten off.

SHAPING FOR LEFT FOOT
Count 11 sts from left-hand side of work and join yarn in eleventh stitch. Repeat Rows 1–5 as for right foot shaping. Fasten off.

Finishing

With RS facing, match center Top with center Base and pin. To create flap for toggle, start sewing from two star stitches down and then sew Top around bootee.

Sew toggle button onto side back.

TOGGLE LOOP
Pick up 1 st at front side corresponding with toggle, make 8ch, join with a ss in first ch.

Fasten off.

Sew in ends.

Star Stitch Bootees

YARN AND MATERIALS

Debbie Bliss Rialto DK (100% merino wool; approx. 105m/115yd per 50g/1¾oz ball) DK (light worsted) weight yarn

1 ball each of shades:
09 Apple (green) (A)
02 Ecru (off-white) (B)

HOOKS AND EQUIPMENT

3.5mm (US size E/4) crochet hook

Yarn needle

TENSION

Exact tension is not essential for this project, just adjust the hook size as necessary to achieve a firm fabric.

SIZE

To fit age: approx 12–36 months

FINISHED MEASUREMENTS

Length from crown to edge: 17.5cm (7in)
Circumference: 45–50cm (18–20in)

ABBREVIATIONS

ch	chain
dc	double crochet
htr	half treble
rep	repeat
ss	slip stitch
st(s)	stitch(es)
yoh	yarn over hook

SPECIAL ABBREVIATIONS

CL (cluster): yoh, insert hook in st, yoh, pull yarn through, yoh, insert hook in same st, yoh, pull yarn through, yoh, insert hook in same st, yoh, pull yarn through, yoh (7 loops on hook), pull yarn through all 7 loops on hook, yoh, 1ch (1 cluster made)

htr2tog (half treble 2 stitches together): *yoh, insert hook in next st, yoh, pull yarn through (3 loops on hook). Without finishing st, rep from * in next st (5 loops on hook), yoh, pull yarn through all 5 loops on hook

Baby Pompom Hat

This very cute hat is made with a super 100% merino yarn so it will not irritate delicate skin. It's such an easy hat to crochet that it can be made over one evening.

Hat

Using A, make 76ch.
Row 1: 1dc in next ch from hook, 1dc in each ch to end.
Rows 2–3: 1ch, 1dc in each st to end.
Row 4: 1ch, 1dc in each of next 5 sts, 2dc in next st, *1dc in each of next 4 sts, 2dc in next st; rep from * to last 5 sts, 1dc in each of next 5 sts. (*90 sts*)
Row 5: 1dc in each st to end. (*90 sts*)
Change to B.
Rows 6–7: 1dc in each st. (*90 sts*)
Change to A.
Rows 8–9: 1dc in each st. (*90 sts*)
Change to B.
Row 10: 3ch, *1CL in next st, miss 1 st; rep from * to last st, 1htr.
Change to A.
Rows 11–12: 2ch, 1htr in each st to end.
Row 13: 2ch, *1htr in each of next 7 sts, htr2tog; rep from * to end. (*80 sts*)
Change to B.
Row 14: 3ch, miss first st, *1CL in next st, miss 1 st; rep from * to last st, 1htr.
Change to A.
Row 15: 1ch, 1dc in each st to end.
Row 16: 2ch, *1htr in each of next 6 sts, htr2tog; rep from * to end. (*70 sts*)
Row 17: 2ch, *1htr in each st to end.
Row 18: 2ch, *1htr in each of next 5 sts, htr2tog; rep from * to end. (*60 sts*)
Row 19: 2ch, *1htr in each st to end.
Row 20: 2ch, *1htr in each of next 4 sts, htr2tog; rep from * to end. (*50 sts*)
Row 21: Rep Row 19.
Row 22: 2ch, htr2tog, *1htr in each of next 3 sts, htr2tog; rep from * to end. (*40 sts*)
Row 23: 2ch, *1htr in each of next 2 sts, htr2tog; rep from * to end. (*30 sts*)
Row 24: 2ch, *htr2tog, 1htr in next st; rep from * to end. (*20 sts*)
Fasten off leaving a long tail approx 30cm (12in).

Finishing

Sew in ends.

Make a running stitch around last row. Pull yarn tight and gather top together, then sew in securely.

Oversew seam together.

POMPOM

Using A and B together, wrap the yarn around two or three fingers approx 80 times. Gently slide the yarn off your fingers and tie a knot in the center very securely. The pompom will now have loops on either side of the knot. Cut all the loops; trim and fluff the pompom into shape and sew onto top of hat.

Nursery Coat Hangers

Show off your beautiful baby clothes on these cute hangers. They're much too nice to keep inside a wardrobe.

YARN AND MATERIALS

Debbie Bliss Rialto DK (100% merino wool, 105m/115yd per 50g/1¾oz) ball) DK (light worsted) weight yarn

Watermelons hanger:
1 ball each of shades:
57 Banana (yellow) (A)
09 Apple (green) (B)
Small amounts of shades:
12 Scarlet (red) (C)
02 Ecru (off-white) (D)
03 Black (E)

Chickens hanger:
1 ball each of shades:
09 Apple (green) (F)
82 Mallard (blue-green) (G)
Small amounts of shades:
02 Ecru (off-white) (H)
37 Earth (brown) (I)
57 Banana (yellow) (J)
12 Scarlet (red) (K)

35 x 20cm (14 x 8in) piece of wadding (enough for two hangers)

2 wooden coat hangers, approx. 31cm (12½in) long

HOOKS AND EQUIPMENT

3.5mm (US size E/4) crochet hook

Yarn needle

FINISHED MEASUREMENTS

Length: 31cm (12½in)

TENSION

Exact tension is not essential for this project, just adjust the hook size as necessary to achieve a firm fabric.

ABBREVIATIONS

ch	chain
dc	double crochet
dtr	double treble
htr	half treble
rep	repeat
ss	slip stitch
st(s)	stitch(es)
tr	treble
yoh	yarn over hook

SPECIAL ABBREVIATIONS

2ch picot: 2ch ss in second ch from hook, pull tight
3ch picot: 3ch, ss in third ch from hook, pull tight
trCL (treble cluster): *yoh, insert hook through ring, yoh, pull yarn through 2 loops (2 loops on hook); rep from * twice more (4 loops on hook), yoh, pull yarn through all 4 loops (1 treble cluster made)

Cover (both hangers)

Using A or F, make 14ch.
Row 1: 3ch (counts as first tr), 1tr in fifth ch from hook, 1tr in each ch to end, turn.
Row 2: 3ch (counts as first tr), 1tr in each tr to last st, 1tr in top of previous 3-ch, turn.
Row 3: Rep Row 2 another 27 times or until work is long enough to cover coat hanger.
Fasten off.

Large leaf (both hangers)

(make 2 or more)
Using B (for Watermelon hanger) or G (for Chickens hanger), make 12ch.
Row 1: 1dc in third ch from hook, 1htr in next st, 1tr in each of next 6 sts, 1htr in next st, dc in end ch.
Row 2: 2ch, working down other side of base chain, 1dc in first st, 1htr in next st, 1tr in each of next 6 sts, 1htr in next st, 1ch, ss into next ch.
Fasten off.

Watermelon hanger

SMALL WATERMELON CHUNKS

(make 9)
Using C, 4ch, 2tr in first ch.
Fasten off.
Join in D, 1ch, 1dc in top of first tr, 2dc in second tr, 1dc in top of fourth ch.
Fasten off.
Join in B, 1ch, 2dc in each of next 4 sts.
Fasten off.
Using E, hand sew 3 sts on each chunk.

LARGE WATERMELON CHUNKS

(make 2)
Using C, 4ch, 1htr, 2tr, 1htr in first ch.
Fasten off.
Join in D, 1ch, 1dc in top of first st, 2dc into each of next 4 sts, ss into second of 4-ch from previous row. (9 sts)
Fasten off.
Join in B, miss 1 st, 2dc in each of next 8 sts. (16 sts)
Fasten off.
Using E, hand sew 3 sts on each chunk.

SMALL LEAF

(make 18)
Using B, make 10ch,
Row 1: 1dc in third ch from hook, 1htr in next st, 1tr in each of next 4 sts, 1htr in next st, 1dc in end ch.
Row 2: 2ch, working down other side of base chain, 1dc in first st, 1htr in next st, 1tr in next 4 sts, 1htr in next st, 1ch, ss in next ch.
Fasten off.

Chickens hanger

HENS

(make 3)
Using H, make 4ch.
Row 1: 5tr into first ch, turn.
Row 2: 3ch, 2tr in each of next 2 sts, 1tr in each of next 2 sts, 2tr in next st, 1tr in last st, turn.
Row 3: 3ch, 1dtr in first st, 1tr in next st, 1htr in next st, ss in each of next 4 sts, 2ch, 3ch picot, 1dtr in same st, 3ch picot, 1tr in next st, 3ch picot, 2ch, ss in last st.
Fasten off.
Rejoin yarn in top of htr on hen's head.
2ch, 1tr in each of next 2 sts, 2ch, ss into same st.
Fasten off.
Legs:
Using I and with RS facing, join yarn to middle of bottom edge of hen's body.
*3ch, [2ch picot] twice, ss in first ch of 2-ch; rep from * once more, ss back in bottom edge.
Fasten off.
Beak:
Join J to bottom of 2ch, 2ch picot.
Fasten off.
Under beak:
Join K to top of 3ch, 3ch picot.
Fasten off.
Comb:
Join K to top of head, [3ch picot] twice, ss in top of head.
Fasten off.

CHICKS

(make 6)
Using H, make 9ch.
Ss into sixth ch from hook, 1trCL into first ch, 3ch ss into first ch.
Fasten off.
Feet:
Using I and with RS facing, join yarn to middle of bottom edge of chick's body. *4ch, ss into second ch, ss into first ch; rep from * once, ss back in bottom edge.
Fasten off.

SMALL FLOWERS
(make 2)
Make 4ch, join with ss to make a ring, 6dc in ring.
*Ss into first dc, 3ch, 1tr into same st, 3ch, ss into same st; rep from * 5 times. (*6 petals*)
Fasten off.

Finishing

Cover wooden part of coat hanger with a layer of wadding to pad.

Place crocheted cover around wadding and work dc to join along bottom edge.

Fasten off.

Sew in ends on all crochet pieces.

Watermelon cover edging and hook embellishments

Join B to one end of bottom of coat hanger cover, make 4ch.

Put hook through middle of top of small watermelon chunk, pull yarn through and make fifth ch, make 4ch. Measure 3cm (1¼in) along bottom of hanger and join ch to cover with dc. Repeat to add remaining small chunks.

Fasten off.

LOOPS
Using B, join yarn in work near base of hook. Make 30ch, ss back in work near hook, make 25ch, ss back in work near hook, make 27ch, ss back in work near hook.

Fasten off.

LEAVES
Place leaves at base of coat hanger hook and stitch in position. Stitch large watermelon chunks between leaves.

Sew in ends.

Chicken cover edging and hook embellishments

Using I, embroider eyes on hen and chicks.
Join 1 hen, 3 chicks, 1 hen, 3 chicks, 1 hen together in order.

Join G to one end of bottom edge of coat hanger cover, ss through tail of hen, *make 12ch, ss through comb of same hen and back in base of coat hanger 6cm (2½in) from end of hanger. Make 8ch, ss in bottom edge of coat hanger cover approx 9cm (3½in) from end, make 8ch, ss in next hen tail and back in bottom edge of coat hanger cover; rep from * twice more.

Fasten off.

LEAVES

Place leaves at base of coat hanger hook and stitch in position, then place flowers on top of leaves around base of the coat hanger hook and stitch in position.

Sew in ends.

Ophelia Buggy Blanket

Just large enough to tuck in the toes, this is the perfect size for a buggy or car seat blanket. The color combinations are light and bright, which make it a suitable blanket for either a boy or a girl.

YARN AND MATERIALS

Valley Yarns Superwash DK (100% merino wool; approx. 125m/137yd per 50g/1¾oz ball) DK (light worsted) weight yarn
 1 ball each of shades:
 01 Natural (off white)
 15 Blue Mist (blue-green)
 09 Wild Rose (bright pink)
 23 Light Blue (pale blue)
 22 Pink (pale pink)
 13 Forest (green)
 10 Soft Yellow (yellow)
 07 Red (red)
 31 Eggplant (dark purple)
 24 Passion Plum (mid purple)
 19 Misty Lilac (light purple)

HOOKS AND EQUIPMENT

4.5mm (US size G/6) crochet hook

Yarn needle

TENSION

15 sts x 8 rows over 10cm (4in) square working treble using a 4.5mm (US size G/6) hook and Valley Yarns Superwash DK.

FINISHED SIZE

Approx. 50 x 62.5cm (20 x 25in)

ABBREVIATIONS

ch	chain
dc	double crochet
htr	half treble
rep	repeat
RS	right side
ss	slip stitch
st(s)	stitch(es)
tr	treble
tr3tog	treble 3 stitches together
yoh	yarn over hook

Blanket

Change color on each row.
Using first color, make 83ch.
Row 1: 1tr in 2nd ch from hook, 1tr in next ch, *1tr in each of next 3 ch, tr3tog over next 3ch, 1tr in next 3-ch, 3tr in next ch; rep from * ending last rep with 2tr in last ch, turn.
Row 2: 3ch, 1tr in first st, *1tr in each of next 3 sts, tr3tog over next 3 sts, 1tr in each of next 3 sts, 3tr in next st; rep from * ending last rep with 2tr in top of 3-ch, turn. Change color.
Rep Row 2 another 48 times more, making a total of 50 rows.
Fasten off.

Edging

Round 1: With RS facing, join A in fasten off st.

SIDE 1 (TOP)

1ch, 1dc in each of next 2 sts, 1htr in each of next 2 sts, 1tr in each of next 3 sts, 1htr in each of next 2 sts, *1dc in next 3 sts, 1htr in each of next 2 sts, 1tr in each of next 3 sts, 1htr in each of next 2 sts; rep from * to last 2 sts, 1dc in next st, 4dc in corner st.

SIDE 2
*Make 2dc in each color down side, 4dc in corner st.

SIDE 3
Working on bottom chain of Row 1 of blanket, 1tr in each of next 2 sts, 1htr in each of next 2 sts; rep from * from Side 1 to last 6 sts, 1dc in each of next 3 sts, 1htr in each of next 2 sts, 1tr in next st, 4dc in corner st.

SIDE 4
Rep Side 2 to last st, make 4dc in corner st, ss in first ch from Side 1.
Fasten off.
Round 2: Using B, make 1dc in each st around blanket, making 4dc in each corner st, join with a ss in first st.
Round 3: Rep Round 2.
Fasten off.

Finishing

Sew in ends.

POMPOMS
(make 4)
Using C, wrap the yarn around three or four fingers approx. 80 times. Gently slide the yarn off your fingers and tie a knot in the center very securely. The pompom will now have loops on either side of the knot. Cut all the loops; trim and fluff the pompom into shape.

Sew one pompom onto each corner of the blanket.

Ophelia Buggy Blanket

CHAPTER 3
Bits and Bobs

YARN AND MATERIALS

Debbie Bliss Baby Cashmerino (55% wool, 33% acrylic, 12% cashmere; 125m/136yd per 50g/1¾oz ball) lightweight DK (sport) weight yarn

1 part ball each of shades:
601 Baby Pink (A)
59 Mallard (dark blue) (B)
02 Apple (light green) (C)
101 Ecru (off-white) (D)
06 Candy Pink (pink) (E)
204 Baby Blue (F)
306 Flame (red) (G)
03 Mint (green) (H)

HOOKS AND EQUIPMENT

3mm (US size D/3) crochet hook

Yarn needle

TENSION

20 sts x 24 rows over a 10cm (4in) square, working double crochet using 3mm (US size D/3) hook and Debbie Bliss Baby Cashmerino yarn or similar.

FINISHED MEASUREMENTS

Approx. 9 x 15cm (3½ x 6in)

NOTE

To fit your own phone, you can change the number of sts and/or rows. The multiple is any number of sts (+ 1 for the base ch).

ABBREVIATIONS

approx.	approximate(ly)
ch	chain
dc	double crochet
rep	repeat
RS	right side
ss	slip stitch
st(s)	stitch(es)
tr	treble

Striped Phone Cosy

This cosy fits a larger mobile phone, and is nice and bright and easy to find in a bag! Here I've used Debbie Bliss Baby Cashmerino yarn as I love the colours, but this is a perfect project for using up scraps of anything similar, as it requires very little yarn.

Cosy

This is made in one piece.
Make 1 row stripes using A, B, C, D, E, F, G, H, changing colour on each row.
Row 1: Using any colour make 21ch, 1dc in second ch from hook and each ch to end. (*20 sts*)
Cut yarn, do not fasten off.
Row 2: Join next colour, 1ch, 1dc in each st to end. (*20 sts*)
Cut yarn, do not fasten off.
Repeat Row 2 until 72 rows have been worked or to required length.
Fasten off.
Sew in ends.

Bow

(make one)

Using D, make 16ch, join with a ss to form a ring.

Round 1 (RS): 1ch (does not count as a st), 1dc in each ch to end, join with a ss in first dc. (*16 sts*)

Round 2: 3ch, (counts as tr), 1tr in each st to end; join with a ss in top of first 3-ch. (*16 sts*)

Round 3: 1ch, 1dc in each st to end, join with a ss in first dc.

Fasten off leaving a tail of approx. 45cm (17½in).

Finishing

With RS together fold Cosy in half lengthways and sew up side seams.

Block and press.

Turn Bow RS out and hold flat with fasten off st and tail at the top at the front centre. Using yarn tail, wrap yarn around centre of ring tightly to create bow shape, then secure in place on one side of cosy approx. 6 rows from the top, using a yarn sewing needle.

Jam Jar Tea Light Cosies

These are perfect over little jam jars holding tea lights. They are made using a fine lace yarn and a lace stitch, so that when the candlelight glows through it creates gorgeous textured patterns.

YARN AND MATERIALS

Lana Grossa Cool Wool Lace (100% merino; approx. 400m/437yd per 50g/1¾oz ball) laceweight yarn

1 part ball each of shades:
46 Pink (bright pink)
52 Pale Pink (pink)
14 Off White (off-white)
50 Lobster (salmon)
48 Azure Blue (deep aqua)
63 Mustard (yellow)

HOOKS AND EQUIPMENT

2.5mm (US size C/2) crochet hook

Yarn needle

TENSION

26 sts x 12 rows over a 10cm (4in) square, working treble crochet using 2.5mm (US size C/2) hook and Lana Grossa Cool Wool Lace.

FINISHED MEASUREMENTS

To fit a 190ml (6.5fl oz) round jam jar

ABBREVIATIONS

approx. approximate(ly)
ch chain
dc double crochet
rep repeat
RS right side
sp space
ss slip stitch
st(s) stitch(es)
tr treble
tch turning chain
tr3tog treble 3 stitches together
yrh yarn round hook

SPECIAL ABBREVIATIONS

3trCL (3 treble cluster): yrh, insert hook in sp, yrh, pull yarn through work (3 loops on hook). Yrh, pull yarn through 2 loops on hook (2 loops on hook). Yrh, insert hook in same sp, yrh, pull yarn through work (4 loops on hook). Yrh, pull yarn through 2 loops on hook (3 loops on hook). Yrh, insert hook in same sp, yrh, pull yarn through work (5 loops on hook). Yrh, pull yarn through 2 loops on hook (4 loops on hook). Yrh, pull yarn through all 4 loops on hook (1 loop on hook).

4trCL (4-treble cluster, made over 2 sps): yrh, insert hook in sp, yrh, pull yarn through work (3 loops on hook). Yrh, pull yarn through first two loops on hook (2 loops on hook). Yrh, insert hook in same sp, yrh pull yarn through work (4 loops on hook). Yrh, pull yarn through first two loops on hook (3 loops on hook). Yrh, insert hook in next sp, yrh, pull yarn though (5 loops on hook). Yrh, pull yarn through first two loops on hook (4 loops on hook). Yrh, insert hook in same sp, yrh, pull yarn through work (6 loops on hook). Yrh, pull yarn through first two loops on hook (5 loops on hook). Yrh, pull yarn through all 5 loops on hook (1 loop on hook).

Cosy

(make 1 in each colour)

BOTTOM EDGING

Row 1: Make 45ch, 1dc in second ch from hook, 1dc in each ch to end. (*44 sts*)

Row 2: 1ch, 1dc in each st to end. (*44 sts*)

Row 3 (increase row): 1ch, *1dc in each of next 8 sts, 2dc in next st; rep from * to last 8 sts, 1dc in each of next 7 sts, 2dc in last st. (*49 sts*)

MAIN PATTERN

Row 1 (RS): 1ch, 1dc in first st, 1dc in next st, *4ch, 4trCL over next 5 sts as follows; leaving last loop of each st on hook work 1tr into each of next 2 sts, miss 1 st, 1tr in each of next 2 sts, yrh and draw through all 5 loops on hook; 4ch, 1dc in next st **, 1ch miss 1 st, 1dc in next st; rep from * ending last rep at **, 1dc in last st.

Row 2: 3ch (counts as 1tr), 1tr in first st, *3ch, 1dc in next 4-ch sp, 1ch, miss CL, 1dc in next 4-ch sp, 3ch, miss 1dc **, 3trCL in next 1ch sp; rep from * ending last rep at **, tr2tog in last dc.

Row 3: 1ch, 1dc in first st, *1dc in next ch sp, 4ch, 4trCL as follows: leaving last loop of each st on hook work 2tr in same ch sp, miss [1dc, 1ch, 1dc], 2tr in next ch sp, yrh and draw through all 5 loops on hook; 4ch, 1dc in same ch sp **, 1ch, rep from * ending last rep at **, 1dc in top of 3-ch from previous row.

Rep Rows 2 and 3 three times more and then rep Row 2 once more.

TOP EDGING

Row 1: 1ch, 3dc in first ch sp, miss 1 dc, 1dc in next 1-ch sp, miss 1 dc, [3dc in next 4-ch sp] twice, miss 1 dc, 1dc in next 1-ch sp, miss 1 dc, *3dc in next ch sp, 3dc in next ch sp, miss 1 dc, 1dc in next 1-ch sp, miss 1 dc; rep from * 3 times more, 3dc in last ch sp, 1dc in top of tr2tog from previous row, 1dc in top of tch. (*44 sts*)

Rows 2–5: 1ch, 1dc in each st. (*44 sts*)

Work more dc rows to top lip of jar if necessary.

Fasten off

Finishing

With RS together, join seam.

Turn RS out and fit over jar.

Bunting

Brighten up any room of the house with some traditional bunting! The flowers between the flags give it a wonderfully feminine feel, and you can use any DK (light worsted) weight yarn for this project.

MATERIALS

Hayfield Bonus DK (100% acrylic; approx. 280m/306yd per 100g/3½oz ball) DK (light worsted) weight yarn

1 ball each of shades:
588 Mauve Marl (pink) (A)
959 Lilac (lilac) (B)
882 Lime (green) (C)
998 Turquoise (blue) (D)
647 Burnt Orange (orange) (E)
957 Primrose (yellow) (F)

HOOKS AND EQUIPMENT

4mm (US size G/6) crochet hook

Yarn needle

TENSION

Each flag measures approx. 18.5cm (7¼in) along each side using a 4mm (US size G/6) hook and Hayfield Bonus DK.

FINISHED MEASUREMENTS

111cm (43½in) long, excluding the ties

ABBREVIATIONS

ch	chain
cont	continu(e)ing
dc	double crochet
rep	repeat
RS	right side
sp(s)	space(s)
ss	slip stitch
st(s)	stitch(es)
tr	treble

Flags

(make 6, using any three of the six colours – A, B, C, D, E and F – for each)

Using first colour, make 4ch, join with a ss in first ch to form a ring.

Round 1 (RS): 3ch (counts as 1tr), 3tr in ring, *[3ch, 4tr in ring] twice, 3ch, join with a ss in top of first 3-ch.
Fasten off first colour.
Cont in rounds with RS always facing.

Round 2: Join second colour with a ss in any 3-ch sp, 3ch (counts as 1tr), [4tr, 1ch, 5tr] in same sp, *1ch, [5tr, 1ch, 5tr] in next 3ch sp; rep from * once more, 1ch, join with a ss in top of first 3-ch.
Fasten off second colour.

Round 3: Join third colour with a ss in 1-ch sp between any two 5-tr corner groups, 3ch (counts as 1 tr), [1tr, 2ch, 2tr] in same sp, *1tr in each of next 5 tr, miss 1ch sp, 1tr in each of next 5 tr, [2tr, 2ch, 2tr] in next 1ch sp (corner); rep from * once more, 1tr in each of next 5 tr, miss 1ch sp, 1tr in each of next 5 tr, join with a ss in top of first 3-ch. Do not fasten off, but cont working with third colour to complete flag.

Round 4: 1ss in next tr, 1ss in next 2-ch sp (corner), 3ch (counts as 1tr), [2tr, 3ch, 3tr] in same sp, *miss 1 tr, [3tr in next tr, miss 2 tr] 4 times, 3tr in next tr, [3tr, 3ch, 3tr] in next 2-ch sp (corner); rep from * once more, miss 1 tr, [3tr in next tr, miss next 2 tr] 4 times, 3tr in next tr, join with a ss in top of first 3-ch.

Round 5: 1ss in each of next 2 tr, 1ss in next 3-ch sp (corner), 3ch (counts as 1tr), [2tr, 3ch, 3tr] in same sp, *3tr in each of next 6 sps between 3-tr groups, [3tr, 3ch, 3tr] in next 3-ch corner sp; rep from * once more, 3tr in each of next 6 sps between 3-tr groups, join with a ss in top of first 3-ch.

Round 6: 1ch, 1dc in same place as last ss, 1dc in each of next 2 tr, 3dc in next 3-ch sp (corner), [1dc in each of next 24 tr, 3dc in next 3-ch sp] twice, 1dc in each of next 21 tr, join with a ss in first dc, 1ss in each of next 2 dc. Fasten off.

TOP EDGE

With RS of first flag facing and using A, join yarn with a ss in centre dc of any 3-dc corner group of first flag, 1ch, 1dc in same place as ss, *1dc in each dc up to next 3-dc corner group, 1dc in each of first 2 dc of group, take next flag and with RS facing, work 1dc in centre dc of any 3-dc corner group (this joins flags together); rep from * until all flags are attached. Do not fasten off, but cont to work first tie as follows.

Ties

FIRST TIE

Cont with A, make approx 59ch or until tie measures 30.5cm (12in) from edge of last flag.
Fasten off.

SECOND TIE

With RS facing, join A with a ss in top of first dc at start of top edge, make approx 59ch or until chain measures 30.5cm (12in) to match first tie.
Fasten off.

Flowers

(make 7, using any two of the six colours – A, B, C, D, E and F – for each)
Using first colour, make 6ch, join with a ss in first dc to form a ring.
Round 1: 1ch, 15dc in ring, enclosing yarn tail inside each dc around ring. Break off first colour, but do not fasten off.
Round 2: Join in second colour with 1ss in first dc in Round 1, *3ch, 1tr in each of next 2 dc, 3ch, 1ss in next dc st; rep from * 4 more times, working last ss in first dc. (5 petals)
Fasten off.
Pull yarn tail to close up centre hole and sew in ends.

Finishing

Press and starch each flag.

Sew on flowers along top of bunting – one between each pair of flags and one at each end.

Tip

The pattern is for a two-colour flower; for a one-colour flower in the centre, do not fasten off on Round 1 but continue to use A for Round 2.

Pin Cushions

These little pin cushions are just perfect for keeping pins and sewing needles safe. Choose any wool-rich DK (light worsted) from your stash as these take very little yarn, but you may need to adjust the size of the lining pieces. I use natural wadding for the lining instead of fabric, because this makes it easier to push in pins or wool sewing needles.

YARN AND MATERIALS

Any part balls of DK (light worsted) yarn, preferably a wool-rich blend

Pin cushion 1
Small amounts of:
Off-white (A/B)
Pink (C)
Pale green/Eau de nil (D/F)
Citrus green (E)

Pin cushion 2
Small amounts of:
Mustard yellow (A/C)
Deep pink (B)
Pale green/Eau de nil (D)
Pink (E)
Blue-green (F)

Pin cushion 3
Small amounts of:
Mustard yellow (A)
Pink (B)
Deep pink (C)
Light blue (D/F)
Pale green/Eau de nil (E)

2 x approx. 12cm (4¾in) squares of thin cotton fabric or natural wadding and matching sewing thread

Small amount of toy stuffing

HOOKS AND EQUIPMENT

4mm (US size G/6) crochet hook

Yarn needle

Sewing needle and thread to match lining material

TENSION

Front and back pieces (before edging is added) measure approx. 7cm (2¾in) square using 4mm (US size G/6) hook.

FINISHED MEASUREMENTS

Approx 11.5cm (4½in) square, including edging

ABBREVIATIONS

ch	chain
cont	continu(e)ing
dc	double crochet
htr	half treble
rep	repeat
RS	right side
sp(s)	space(s)
ss	slip stitch
st(s)	stitch(es)
tr	treble
WS	wrong side

SPECIAL ABBREVIATION

PC (popcorn): work 5tr in next st, pull up the loop of 5th tr slightly and remove hook, then insert hook in top of first tr, reinsert hook in dropped loop of 5th tr (2 loops on hook), pull fifth tr through first tr and pull firmly

54 *Bits and Bobs*

Front

Using A, make 4ch, join with a ss in first ch to form a ring.
Round 1 (RS): 1ch, 8dc in ring, break off A (see Tip), join B with a ss in first dc.
Cont in rounds with RS always facing.
Round 2: 3ch, 1PC in same dc as last ss, 2ch, [1PC in next dc, 2ch] 7 times, join with a ss in top of first PC. (8 petals)
Fasten off B.
Round 3: Join C with a ss in any 2ch sp, 3ch (counts as first tr), [2tr, 1ch, 3tr] in same sp, 1ch, 3tr in next 2ch sp, *1ch, [3tr, 1ch, 3tr] in next 2ch sp, 1ch, 3tr in next ch sp; rep from * twice more, 1ch, join with a ss in top of first 3-ch.
Fasten off.

Back

Using D, make 4ch, join with a ss to first ch to form a ring.
Round 1 (RS): 3ch, 2tr in ring, 2ch, [3tr in ring, 2ch] 3 times, join with a ss in top of first 3-ch.
Cont in rounds with RS always facing.
Round 2: 1ss in each of next 2 tr, 1ss in next 2ch sp, 3ch, [2tr, 1ch, 3tr] in same sp, *1ch, [3tr, 1ch, 3tr] in next 2ch sp; rep from * twice more, 1ch, join with a ss in top of first 3-ch.
Round 3: 1ss in each of next 2 tr, 1ss in next 1-ch sp, 2ch (counts as first htr), [2htr, 1ch, 3htr] in same 1-ch sp, 1ch, 3htr in next 1-ch sp, 1ch, *[3htr, 1ch, 3htr] in next 1-ch sp, 1ch, 3htr in next 1-ch sp, 1ch; rep from * twice more, join with a ss in top of first 3-ch.
Fasten off.

Finishing

Sew in ends.

FABRIC PILLOW

With WS together, sew two fabric squares together, taking a 1.5cm (⅝in) seam allowance and leaving small opening in one side. Turn RS out, fill very firmly with toy stuffing and sew opening closed.

JOIN FRONT AND BACK

With Front and Back WS together, front facing upwards and working through both pieces, join E in any corner sp, 1ch, 2dc in same sp, *1dc in each st and ch sp to next corner, 2dc in corner; rep from * twice more, insert fabric pillow, 1dc in each st and ch sp to next corner (enclosing pillow), join with a ss in first dc.
Fasten off E.

Edging

With front facing upwards, join F with a ss in 2nd st to right of any 2dc corner group, 5tr in 2nd dc of next 2dc corner group, *miss 1 dc, 1ss in next dc, [miss 1dc, 5tr in next dc, miss 1 dc, 1ss in next dc] twice, 5tr in 2nd dc of next 2dc corner group; rep from * twice, miss 1 dc, 1ss in next dc, [miss 1 dc, 5tr in next dc, miss 1 dc, 1ss in next dc] twice, working last ss in same place as first ss.
Fasten off.

Pin Cushions

Crochet Hook Cosy

At home I keep my crochet hooks in jam jars, but when I go out I like to take a portable crochet hook cosy and this is just the perfect size. It's made in the round, using spirals, and with a set of crochet hooks inside, it would make a great gift for someone.

YARN AND MATERIALS

Debbie Bliss Rialto DK (100% merino wool; approx. 105m/115yd) per 50g/1¾oz) ball) DK (light worsted) weight yarn

  1 ball each in shades:
  72 Ocean (blue) (A)
  02 Ecru (off-white) (B)

1 small button

HOOKS AND EQUIPMENT

3mm (US size D/3) crochet hook

Stitch marker

Yarn needle

TENSION

20 sts x 22 rows over a 10cm (4in) square, working double crochet using 3mm (US size D/3) hook and Debbie Bliss Rialto DK yarn.

FINISHED MEASUREMENTS

Approx. 5.5 x 20cm (2¼ x 8in)

ABBREVIATIONS

approx.	approximately
BLO	back loop only
ch	chain
cont	continu(e)ing
dc	double crochet
dc2tog	double crochet 2 together
ss	slip stitch
st(s)	stitch(es)

Cosy

Using A, make 2ch, 6dc in second ch from hook. Place a stitch marker in loop on hook.

Round 1: 2dc in each st to end. (*12 sts*)
Round 2: 2dc in each st to end. (*24 sts*)
Rounds 3–4: 1dc in BLO of each st to end. (*24 sts*)

Work should now look like a small bowl curving inwards. Turn work out so that ridges formed by working in back loops are on outside.
Cont to work on this side of work.

Round 5: Working in both loops of each st, 1dc in each st to end. (*24 sts*)

Cont working 1dc in each st, in a spiral, until work measures approx. 17cm (6¾in) or until piece is same size as length of crochet hooks.
Turn, then begin working in rows.

Next 12 rows: 1ch, 1dc in each of next 13 sts. (*13 sts*)
Next row: 1ch, dc2tog, 1dc in each of next 9 sts, dc2tog. (*11 sts*)
Next row: 1ch, 1dc in each st to end. (*11 sts*)
Next row: 1ch, dc2tog, 1dc in each of next 7 sts, dc2tog. (*9 sts*)
Next row: 1ch, 1dc in each st to end. (*9 sts*)
Next row: 1ch, dc2tog, 1dc in each of next 5 sts, dc2tog. (*7 sts*)
Next row (buttonhole): 1ch, dc2tog, 2ch, miss next 3 sts, dc2tog.
Next row: 1ch, 2dc in ch sp, ss in last st. (*4 sts*)
Cut yarn, do not fasten off.

EDGING
Join B, 1ch, make approx. 21dc down first side, 1dc in each st along front edge, make approx. 25dc along second side and top to join. Join with a ss in first dc.
Fasten off.

Finishing

Sew in ends, then sew on button to match buttonhole.

Flower Brooch

Brooches always make beautiful gifts for friends, as well as being an accessory for yourself. This brooch has a delicate vintage look in a pretty deep lilac, but you could make a whole batch of these, using up your smaller remnants of yarn.

YARN AND MATERIALS

Debbie Bliss Baby Cashmerino (55% wool, 33% acrylic, 12% cashmere; 125m/136yd per 50g/1¾oz ball) lightweight DK (sport) weight yarn
  Small amounts of shades:
  10 Lilac (A)
  18 Citrus (green) (B)
  01 Primrose (yellow) (C)

Small brooch pin

3 x 4mm (size 6) glass beads

HOOKS AND EQUIPMENT

2.5mm (US size C/2) crochet hook

Yarn needle

Sewing needle and sewing thread to match beads

TENSION

Flower layers measure approx 6cm (2½in) in diameter and each leaf is approx 4.5cm (1¾in) long using 2.5mm (US size C/2) hook and Debbie Bliss Baby Cashmerino.

FINISHED MEASUREMENTS

Across the widest part, the brooch measures 9cm (3½in)

ABBREVIATIONS

ch	chain
cont	continu(e)ing
dc	double crochet
dtr	double treble
htr	half treble
rep	repeat
RS	right side
ss	slip stitch
st(s)	stitch(es)
tr	treble
ttr	triple treble

Flower Back

Using A, make 4ch, join with a ss in first ch to form a ring.
Round 1 (RS): 1ch, 8dc in ring, join with a ss in first dc. Cont with RS facing.
Round 2: *5ch, [1ttr, 1dtr, 1tr, 1dtr, 1ttr] in next dc, 5ch, 1ss in next dc; rep from * 3 times more, working last ss in base of first 5-ch.
Fasten off.

Flower Front

Using A, make 4ch, join with a ss in first ch to form a ring.
Round 1 (RS): 1ch, 8dc in ring, join with a ss in first dc. Cont with RS facing.
Round 2: *4ch, 4dtr in next dc, 4ch, 1ss in next dc; rep from * 3 times more, working last ss in base of first 4-ch.
Fasten off

Leaves

(make 3)
Using B, make 8ch.
Round 1 (RS): 1dc in 2nd ch from hook, 1htr in next ch, 1tr in each of next 2 ch, 2tr in next ch, 1htr in next ch, 1dc in next ch, 2ch, turn work so bottom of starting ch is at top and cont along bottom of sts just made, 1dc in first ch, 1htr in next ch, 2tr in next ch, 1tr in each of next 2 ch, 1htr in next ch, 1dc in last ch, join with a ss in tip of leaf.
Fasten off.

Finishing

Sew in ends.

Lay flower front on top of flower back, with RS facing upwards, and sew together at the centre using matching yarn. Using C, embroider four large bullion or French knots in the centre of the flower. Using matching yarn, sew leaves onto back of flower.

Sew three small beads on top of knots, using matching sewing thread.

Sew a brooch pin to the back, using sewing thread.

Butterfly and Blossom Key Ring

These little flowers and butterfly make a very pretty addition to your key ring. They are made in cotton, which is more hard-wearing than wool.

YARN AND MATERIALS

Scraps of any 100% cotton DK (light worsted) weight yarn in:
- Pale yellow-green (A)
- Dark lilac (B)
- Orange (C)
- Bright pink (D)
- Purple (E)
- Pale pink (F)
- Leaf green (G)

HOOKS AND EQUIPMENT

3mm (US size D/3) crochet hook

Sewing needle and matching thread

Key ring

TENSION

Exact tension is not essential for this project.

FINISHED MEASUREMENTS

Group of flowers and butterfly hangs approx. 5cm (2in) long from key ring

ABBREVIATIONS

ch	chain
cont	continu(e)ing
dc	double crochet
dtr	double treble
rep	repeat
RS	right side
ss	slip stitch
st(s)	stitch(es)
tr	treble
yrh	yarn round hook

Tip

Use bright colours for this key ring to make your keys easier to find!

Butterfly Wings

Using A, make 11ch.
Row 1 (RS): 2tr in 4th ch from hook, 2ch, 1dc in next ch, [1tr, 1dtr] in next ch, 3ch, 1ss in 3rd ch from hook (picot), 3ch, 1ss in next ch (first wing complete), 6ch, 1ss in 3rd ch from hook (picot), [1dtr, 1tr] in next ch, 2ch, 1dc in next ch, 2ch, 2tr in next ch, 2ch, 1ss in last ch.
Fasten off.
Sew wings together along centre (chain edge).

Butterfly Body

Using B, make 7ch.
Row 1 (RS): 2dc in 2nd ch from hook, 1ss in each ch to end.
Fasten off.

Flowers

(make 1 each in D, E and F)
Make 4ch, join with a ss in first ch to form a ring.
Round 1 (RS): [5ch, 1ss in ring] 5 times. (5 petals)
Fasten off.

STALK
Using G, join yarn with a ss in two loops at back of flower, make 6ch, break off G leaving approx. 10cm (4in) tail. Remove hook and set loop aside.
Rep on all flowers.

Finishing

Sew on butterfly body in centre of wings.

Using C, embroider a spot in each corner of wing.

To attach flowers, insert hook through smaller of rings on key ring (the larger is for the keys) and into loop of one flower stalk, yrh, pull yarn through loop and through ring.

Fasten off.

Cont to attach each flower to ring.

To attach butterfly, using G, insert hook through ring (same place as flowers), join yarn with a ss in a loop at back of top of butterfly, yrh, pull yarn through loop on hook and through ring.

Fasten off.

Sew in each end along back of each ch of flower and of butterfly, securing butterfly and flowers with ends.

Butterfly and Blossom Key Ring

CHAPTER 4
Toys

Pickle the Puppy

This loveable toy can be made up in any good-quality 100% cotton DK (light worsted) yarn, just experiment with hook size if necessary, until you get a good, solid feel to the work.

YARN AND MATERIALS

You can use any cotton DK (light worsted) yarn for this project
 1 ball of Yellow (A)
 Small amounts of Black and Pink

Pair of safety eyes

Stuffing

Small piece of fabric for the scarf

HOOKS AND EQUIPMENT

4mm (US size G/6) crochet hook

Yarn needle

Sewing needle and thread to match fabric

TENSION

Exact tension is not essential for this project, just adjust the hook size if necessary to achieve a firm fabric.

FINISHED MEASUREMENTS

Approx. 10cm (4in.) tall.

ABBREVIATIONS

ch	chain
dc	double crochet;
dc2tog	double crochet 2 stitches together
rep	repeat
ss	slip stitch
st(s)	stitch(es)

Head

Using A, make 2ch.
Round 1: 6dc in second ch from hook.
Round 2: 2dc in each st. (*12 sts*)
Round 3: *1dc in each of next 2 sts, 2dc in next st; rep from * to end. (*16 sts*)
Round 4: *1dc in each of next 3 sts, 2dc in next st; rep from * to end. (*20 sts*)
Round 5: *1dc in each of next 4 sts, 2dc in next st; rep from * to end. (*24 sts*)
Rounds 6–8: 1dc in each st.
Round 9: *1dc in each of next 2 sts, dc2tog; rep from * to end. (*18 sts*)
Round 10: *1dc in next st, dc2tog; rep from * to end. (*12 sts*)
Insert eyes and secure. Stuff head.
Round 11: *Dc2tog; rep from * until opening is closed.
Fasten off.

Muzzle

Using A, make 2ch.
Round 1: 6dc in second ch from hook.
Round 2: 2dc in each st. (*12 sts*)
Rounds 3–4: 1dc in each st.
Fasten off.
Stuff muzzle lightly. Pin and sew to face. Embroider nose and mouth details using the black yarn.

Ears

(make 2)
Using A, make 2ch.
Round 1: 6dc in second ch from hook.
Round 2: 1dc in each st.
Round 3: 2dc in each st. (*12 sts*)
Rounds 4–5: 1dc in each st.
Round 6: *Dc2tog, 1dc in each of next 4 sts; rep from * once. (*10 sts*)
Fasten off.
Work running stitch around inside edge of ears, up 3 sides only, leaving base open. This defines the shape of the ears. Gently push finger up through opening to open the ears and shape. Pin and sew to head.

Body

Using A, make 2ch.
Round 1: 6dc in second chain from hook.
Round 2: 2dc in each st. (*12 sts*)
Round 3: *1dc in next st, 2dc in next st; rep from * to end. (*18 sts*)
Round 4: *1dc in each of next 2 sts, 2dc in next st; rep from * to end. (*24 sts*)
Round 5: *1dc in each of next 3 sts, 2dc in next st; rep from * to end. (*30 sts*)
Rounds 6–15: 1dc in each st.
Round 16: *1dc in each of next 3 sts, dc2tog; rep from * to end. (*24 sts*)
Round 17: *1dc in each of next 2 sts, dc2tog; rep from * to end. (*18 sts*)
Stuff firmly.
Round 18: *1dc in next st, dc2tog; rep from * to end. (*12 sts*)
Round 19: *Miss 1 st, 1dc in next st; rep from * until opening is closed.
Fasten off, sew in ends.
Pin and sew to head.

Legs
(make 4)
Using A, make 2ch.
Round 1: 5dc in second ch from hook.
Round 2: 2dc in each st. (*10 sts*)
Round 3: 1dc in each st.
Round 4: *1dc in each of next 3 sts, dc2tog; rep from * once. (*8 sts*)
Round 5: 1dc in each st until work measures 7cm (2¾in).
Fasten off.
Stuff. Pin in position and sew to body.

Tail
Using A, make 2ch.
Round 1: 4dc in second ch from hook.
Round 2: 2dc in next st, 1dc in each st to last st, 2dc in last st. (*6 sts*)
Round 3: *1dc in next st, 2dc in next st; rep from * to end. (*9 sts*)
Rounds 4–6: 1dc in each st.
Round 7: *Dc2tog, 1dc in next st; rep from * to end. (*6 sts*)
Rounds 8–9: 1dc in each st.
Fasten off.
Stuff lightly. Pin and sew to body.

Scarf
Use the template on page 94 to cut out scarf. Hem the edges using the sewing needle and matching thread. Tie the scarf around Pickle's neck.

Melody the Kitten

This cute little kitten can be made in any soft wool DK (light worsted) yarn you have in suitable colours. You could even match the colour of the cat to your own pet.

YARN AND MATERIALS
You can use any soft wool DK (light worsted) weight yarn
- 1 part ball in Cream or Off-white (A)
- 1 part ball in Mauve or Deep pink (B)
- Small amounts of:
- Red (C)
- Purple (D)
- Black or black embroidery thread (floss) (E)

Small amount of pale pink felt for the muzzle

Small amount of dark pink felt for the nose

Pair of safety eyes

Stuffing

HOOKS AND EQUIPMENT
4mm (US size G/6) crochet hook

Yarn needle

Sewing needle and thread to match felt

TENSION
Exact tension is not essential for this project, just adjust the hook size if necessary to achieve a firm fabric.

FINISHED MEASUREMENTS
Approx. 10cm (4in) tall.

ABBREVIATIONS
ch	chain
dc	double crochet
dc2tog	double crochet 2 stitches together
htr	half treble
rep	repeat
ss	slip stitch
st(s)	stitch(es)
tr	treble

Head
Using A, make 2ch.
Round 1: 6dc in second ch from hook.
Round 2: 2dc in each st. (*12 sts*)
Round 3: *1dc in next st. 2dc in next st; rep from * to end. (*18 sts*)
Round 4: *1dc in each of next 2 sts. 2dc in next st; rep from * to end. (*24 sts*)
Round 5: *1dc in each of next 3 sts, 2dc in next st; rep from * to end. (*30 sts*)
Round 6: *1dc in each of next 4 sts, 2dc in next st; rep from * to end. (*36 sts*)
Round 7: 1dc in each st.
Round 8: *1dc in each of next 4 sts, dc2tog; rep from * to end. (*30 sts*)
Round 9: *1dc in each of next 3 sts, dc2tog; rep from * to end. (*24 sts*)
Round 10: *1dc in each of next 2 sts, dc2tog; rep from * to end. (*18 sts*)
Round 11: 1dc in each st.
Round 12: *1dc in next st, dc2tog; rep from * to end. (*12 sts*)
Insert eyes in head and secure. Stuff firmly.
Round 13: *Miss 1 st, 1dc in next st; rep from * until opening is closed.
Fasten off.

Body
Using A, make 2ch.
Round 1: 6dc in second ch from hook.
Round 2: 2dc in each st. (*12 sts*)
Round 3: *1dc in next st, 2dc in next st; rep from * to end. (*18 sts*)
Rounds 4–9: 1dc in each st.
Round 10: *1dc in next st, dc2tog; rep from * to end. (*12 sts*)
Fasten off. Stuff. Pin and sew to head.

Arms

(make 2)
Using A, make 2ch.
Round 1: 6dc in second ch from hook.
Round 2: 1dc in each st.
Continue until arms measure 4cm (1½in).
Fasten off.
Do not stuff. Pin and sew to body.

Legs

(make 2)
Using A, make 2ch.
Round 1: 6dc in second ch from hook.
Round 2: 1dc in each st.
Continue until legs measure 4cm (1½in).
Fasten off.
Do not stuff. Pin and sew to body.

Ears

(make 2)
Using A, make 5 ch
Row 1: 1dc in second ch from hook, 1dc in each ch.
Row 2: 1ch, 1dc in each dc.
Rep Row 2 until work forms a square.
Fold square in half to make a triangle and dc sides together, at top point make 2dc.
Fasten off.
Pin and sew to head.

Dress

Using B, make 50ch.

FRILL

Ss in second ch from hook, *miss 1ch, 3tr in next ch, miss 1ch, ss in next ch; rep from * to end.
Then work into other side of ch, so frill edge is facing downward.
Next row: 3ch, *1tr in same ch as 3tr, 1tr in same ch as ss; rep from * to end. (*25 sts*)
Next row: 1ch, 1dc in each st, 1ch, turn.
Rep last row twice.
Next row: Miss 1 st, 1dc in each st to end, 1ch, turn.
Next row: Miss 1 st, 1dc in each st to end.
Fasten off.
Join centre back seam.

STRAPS

The following is a guide to where to place the straps. Depending on your tension this could vary. Fit dress onto kitten and mark with pins where straps should be worked. Using B, *join yarn at one front marker, 7ch, ss in corresponding back marker, 1ch, 1dc in each ch, ss in same place as join.
Fasten off.
Work second strap as first.

Finishing

Embroider a flower below ear, using C for the centre and D for the petals.

Cut out a pale pink felt oval for muzzle. Cut out a dark pink felt triangle for nose and sew to muzzle. Sew muzzle to head.

Using E, embroider mouth detail and whiskers.

Fit dress on kitten.

Sparkles the Snowman

This cute snowman figure will brighten up your Christmas table or mantelpiece. You can use odds and ends of any wool-rich DK (light worsted) weight yarn for this project.

YARN AND MATERIALS

Wool DK (light worsted) weight yarn
  1 part ball each of:
  White (A)
  Light brown (B)
  Scraps in each of:
  Black (C)
  Orange (D)
  Red (E)
  Green (F)

Toy stuffing

Pair of safety eyes

2 bells, optional (not suitable for young children)

HOOKS AND EQUIPMENT

4mm (US size G/6) crochet hook

Sewing needle and thread (for bells)

Yarn needle

TENSION

Exact tension is not essential for this project, just adjust the hook size if necessary to achieve a firm fabric.

FINISHED MEASUREMENT

Approx. 10cm (4in) tall.

ABBREVIATIONS

ch	chain
dc	double crochet
dc2tog	double crochet 2 stitches together
rep	repeat
ss	slip stitch;
st(s)	stitch(es)

Head

Using A, make 2ch.
Round 1: 6dc in second ch from hook.
Round 2: 2dc in each st. (*12 sts*)
Round 3: *1dc in next st, 2dc in next st; rep from * to end. (*18 sts*)
Round 4: *1dc in each of next 2 sts, 2dc in next st; rep from * to end. (*24 sts*)
Round 5: *1dc in each of next 3 sts, 2dc in next st; rep from * to end. (*30 sts*)
Rounds 6–10: 1dc in each st.
Round 11: 1dc in each of next 3 sts, dc2tog; rep from * to end. (*24 sts*)
Round 12: *1dc in each of next 2 sts, dc2tog; rep from * to end. (*18 sts*)
Insert safety eyes and secure. Stuff.
Round 13: *1dc in next st, dc2tog; rep from * to end. (*12 sts*)
Round 14: [Dc2tog] until opening is closed.
Fasten off.

Body

Using A, make 2ch.
Round 1: 6dc in second ch from hook.
Round 2: 2dc in each st. (*12 sts*)
Round 3: *1dc in next st, 2dc in next st; rep from * to end. (*18 sts*)
Round 4: *1dc in each of next 2 sts, 2dc in next st; rep from * to end. (*24 sts*)
Round 5: *1dc in each of next 3 sts, 2dc in next st; rep from * to end. (*30 sts*)
Round 6: *1dc in each of next 4 sts, 2dc in next st; rep from * to end. (*36 sts*)
Rounds 7–14: 1dc in each st.
Round 15: *1dc in each of next 4 sts, dc2tog; rep from * to end. (*30 sts*)
Round 16: *1dc in each of next 3 sts, dc2tog; rep from * to end. (*24 sts*)
Round 17: *1dc in each of next 2 sts, dc2tog; rep from * to end. (*18 sts*)
Round 18: 1dc in each st.
Stuff body firmly.
Round 19: *1dc in next st, dc2tog; rep from * to end. (*12 sts*)
Round 20: *Miss 1st, 1dc in next st; rep from * to end. (*6 sts*)
Fasten off.
Pin and sew to head.
Using C, work three French knots down centre of body for buttons.

Arms

(make 2)
Using A, make 2ch.
Round 1: 6dc in second ch from hook.
Round 2: 1dc in each st.
Continue until arms measure 4cm (1½in).
Fasten off.
Do not stuff. Pin and sew arms to body.

Nose

Using D, make 2ch.
Round 1: 6dc in second ch from hook.
Round 2: 1dc in each st.
Round 3: [Dc2tog] 3 times.
Round 4: *Insert hook into next st and draw up a loop; rep from * twice more, yarn over and draw through all 4 loops.
Fasten off.
Do not stuff. Pin and sew to face.

Face details

Embroider mouth using E.

Scarf

Using F, make 5ch.
Row 1: 1dc in second ch from hook, 1dc in next 3 sts. (*4 sts*)
Row 2: 1ch, 1dc in each st. (*4 sts*)
Join in B.
Row 3: 1ch, 1dc in each st.
Row 4: 1ch, 1dc in each st.
Join in green.
Row 5: 1ch, 1dc in each st.
Rep Rows 3–5 until scarf measures 29cm (11½in)
Fasten off.
Sew a bell on each end. Tie scarf round neck.

Hat

Using B, make 2ch.
Round 1: 6ch in second ch from hook.
Round 2: 2dc in each st. (*12 sts*)
Round 3: *1dc in next st, 2dc in next st; rep from * to end. (*18 sts*)
Rounds 4–6: 1dc in each st.
Round 7: 2dc in each st. (*36 sts*)
Round 8: [Dc2tog] to end. (*18 sts*)
Round 9: *1dc in next st, 2dc in next st; rep from * to end. (*27 sts*)
Round 10: *1dc in each of next 2 sts, 2dc in next st; rep from * to end. (*36 sts*)
Round 11: *1dc in each of next 3 sts, 2dc in next st; rep from * to last st, ss in last st. (*45 sts*)
Fasten off.
Put hat on head and make small stitches into head to secure in place.

Billy the Bear

Billy is a happy bear, made in rounds. He's very squidgy and easy to carry – don't over-stuff him, he should be lovely, soft and cuddly; break the stuffing into small pieces before inserting.

YARN AND MATERIALS

Debbie Bliss Rialto DK (100% merino wool; approx. 105m/115yd per 50g/1¾oz ball) DK (light worsted) weight yarn

    1 ball each of shades:
    02 Ecru (off-white) (A)
    19 Duck Egg (pale blue-green)
    66 Vintage Pink (pale pink)
    82 Mallard (blue-green)
    99 Mustard (yellow)
    12 Scarlet (red)
    09 Apple (green)

Black safety eyes

Fibrefill stuffing

Scrap of black yarn for face details

HOOKS AND EQUIPMENT

3.5mm (US size E/4) crochet hook

Stitch marker

Yarn needle

TENSION

20 sts x 15 rows over a 10cm (4in) square working in double crochet using a 3.5mm (US size E/4) hook and Debbie Bliss Rialto DK.

FINISHED MEASUREMENTS

Length: approx. 34cm (13½in)

ABBREVIATIONS

ch	chain
dc	double crochet
dc2tog	double crochet 2 stitches together
rep	repeat
RS	right side
ss	slip stitch
st(s)	stitch(es)
WS	wrong side
yrh	yarn round hook

Head

Alternate colours every round, except for Rounds 1 and 2 and 25 and 26, which are the same.
Using A, make 2ch.
Round 1: 6dc in second ch from hook. (*6 sts*)
Place st marker at beg of each round (when counting, loop on hook counts as one st).
Round 2: 2dc in each st. (*12 sts*)
Change colour on next and every following round.
Round 3: *1dc in first st, 2dc in next st; rep from * to end. (*18 sts*)
Rounds 4–5: 1dc in each st.
Round 6: *1dc in each of next 2 sts, 2dc in next st; rep from * to end. (*24 sts*)
Rounds 7–8: 1dc in each st. (*24 sts*)
Round 9: 1dc in each of next 7 sts, 2dc in each of next 10 sts, 1dc in each of next 7 sts. (*34 sts*)
Round 10: *1dc in next st, 2dc in next st; rep from * once more, 1dc in each of next 25 sts, 2dc in next st, 1dc in each of next 2 sts, 2dc in next st, 1dc. (*38 sts*)
Round 11: 1dc in each of next 11 sts, 2dc in next st, *1dc in each of next 2 sts, 2dc in next st, rep from * 4 times more, 1dc in each of next 11 sts. (*44 sts*)
Rounds 12–18: 1dc in each st. (*44 sts*)
Round 19: 1dc in next st, dc2tog, 1dc in each of next 2 sts, dc2tog, 1dc in each of next 30 sts, dc2tog, 1dc in next 2 sts, dc2tog, 1dc. (*40 sts*)
Round 20: 1dc in each of next 11 sts, dc2tog, 1dc in next 2 sts, dc2tog, 1dc in each of next 6 sts, dc2tog, 1dc in each of next 2 sts, dc2tog, 1dc in each of next 11 sts. (*36 sts*)
Round 21: 1dc in each st. (*36 sts*)
Round 22: *1dc in each of next 4 sts, dc2tog; rep from * to end. (*30 sts*)

Tip

Use safety eyes or embroider the eyes – the bear may reach little hands or little mouths. Slip stitch at the end of each round in last stitch. To join colours keep the loop on the hook, place the hook in the next stitch and then use the new colour.

Round 23: *1dc in each of next 3 sts, dc2tog; rep * to end. (*24 sts*)
Insert eyes in 9th row from nose and stuff head.
Round 24: *1dc in each of next 2 sts, dc2tog; rep * to end. (*18 sts*)
Round 25: using A, *1dc in next st, dc2tog; rep from * to end. (*12 sts*)
Do not change colour.
Round 26: Dc2tog around. (*6 sts*)
Fasten off with a long tail approx. 15cm (6in).
Finish stuffing head then use yarn needle to thread tail through sts of last round to close gap neatly.
Sew in ends.

Ears

(make 4)
Do not count loop on hook as one st on this section – st marker is not necessary.
Using A, make 2ch, 6dc in second ch from hook (do not join ring), turn. (*6 sts*)
Row 1: 1ch, 1dc in next st, 2dc in each of next 4 sts, 1dc in last st. (*10 sts*)
Row 2: 1ch, 2dc in first st, *1dc in next 2 sts, 2dc in next st; rep from * twice more. (*14 sts*)
Fasten off.
Join ears to head:
Place two ears with WS together, join yarn in one corner by pushing hook through both ears. 1ch, work 1dc around by pushing hook through both ears to join semi-circle top of ears. Ss in bottom corner of semi-circle to join.
Rep with other set of ears.
Fasten off. Sew ears onto head.

Body

Alternate colours every round, except for Rounds 1 and 2 and 30 and 31, which are the same.
Using A, make 2ch.
Round 1: 6dc in second ch from hook, join round and each subsequent round with ss. (*6 sts*)
Round 2: 2dc in each st. (*12 sts*)
Change colour on next and every following round.
Round 3: *1dc in next st, 2dc in next st; rep from * to end. (*18 sts*)
Round 4: *1dc in each of next 2 sts, 2dc in next st; rep from * to end. (*24 sts*)
Rounds 5–7: 1dc in each st. (*24 sts*)
Round 8: 1dc in next st, 2dc in next st, *1dc in each of next 3 sts, 2dc in next st; rep from * to last 2 sts, 1dc in each st. (*30 sts*)
Rounds 9–10: 1dc in each st. (*30 sts*)
Round 11: *1dc in each of next 4 sts, 2dc in next st; rep from * to end. (*36 sts*)
Rounds 12–13: 1dc in each st (*36 sts*)
Round 14: *1dc in each of next 5 sts, 2dc in next st; rep from * to end. (*42 sts*)
Rounds 15–17: 1dc in each st. (*42 sts*)
Round 18: 1dc in each of next 8 sts, 2dc in next st, *1dc in each of next 4 sts, 2dc in next st; rep from * 4 more times, 1dc in each st to end. (*48 sts*)
Rounds 19–22: 1dc in each st. (*48 sts*)
Round 23: 1dc in each of next 3 sts, dc2tog, *1dc in each of next 6 sts, dc2tog; rep from * 4 times more, 1dc in each st to end. (*42 sts*)
Round 24: 1dc in each st. (*42 sts*)

Round 25: 1dc in each of next 4 sts, dc2tog, *1dc in each of next 9 sts, dc2tog; rep from * twice more, 1dc in each of next 3 sts. (*38 sts*)
Round 26: 1dc in each of next 3 sts, dc2tog, *1dc in each of next 8 sts, dc2tog; rep from * twice more, 1dc in each of next 3 sts. (*34 sts*)
Round 27: 1dc in each of next 3 sts, dc2tog, *1dc in each of next 7 sts, dc2tog; rep from * twice more, 1dc in each of next 2 sts. (*30 sts*)
Round 28: 1dc in each st. (*30 sts*)
Round 29: *1dc in each of next 3 sts, dc2tog; rep from * to end. (*24 sts*)
Stuff body.
Round 30: Using A, *1dc in each of next 2 sts, dc2tog; rep from * to end. (*18 sts*)
Do not change colour.
Round 31: *1dc in each of next st, dc2tog; rep from * to end. (*12 sts*)
Round 32: Dc2tog around. (*6 sts*)
Fasten off with a long tail approx. 15cm (6in). Finish stuffing body and use yarn needle to thread tail through sts of last round to close gap neatly.

Legs

(make two)
Using A, make 2ch.
Round 1: 6dc in second ch from hook.
Round 2: 2dc in each st. (*12 sts*)
Round 3: *2dc in first st, 1dc in next st; rep from * to end. (*18 sts*)
Round 4: *2dc in first st, 1dc in each of next 2 sts; rep from * to end. (*24 sts*)
Round 5–6: 1dc in each st. (*24 sts*)
Round 7: *Dc2tog, 1dc in next st; rep from * to end. (*16 sts*)
Round 8: 1dc in each st. (*16 sts*)
Rep Round 8 until work measures approx. 12cm (4½in).
Fasten off.

Arms

(make two)
Rep pattern as for legs.
Fasten off.

Finishing

Sew in ends.
Embroider nose and mouth detail. Pin pieces in place first to check positioning. Sew body to head with widest part at bottom. Stuff legs and arms and attach to body.

Billy the Bear

Sugar Mice

These three little sugar mice can be made from paler pastels if you prefer, but we think they look so appealing in these brighter shades. They are perfect for using up smaller amounts of yarn.

YARN AND MATERIALS

Debbie Bliss Rialto DK (100% merino wool; 105m/115yd per 50g/1¾oz ball) DK (light worsted) weight yarn
- *Mouse 1:* part ball of shade 66 Vintage Pink (soft pink)
- *Mouse 2:* part ball of shade 54 Mint (light green)
- *Mouse 3:* part ball of shade 99 Mustard (yellow)

Small amount of white felt for the nose

White embroidery thread (floss) for the whiskers

Pair safety eyes

Stuffing

HOOKS AND EQUIPMENT

4mm (US size G/6) crochet hook

Yarn needle

Sewing needle

TENSION

Exact tension is not essential for this project, just adjust the hook size if necessary to give you a firm fabric.

FINISHED MEASUREMENTS

Approx. 5cm (2in) tall

ABBREVIATIONS

ch	chain
dc	double crochet
dc2tog	double crochet 2 stitches together
rep	repeat
ss	slip stitch
st(s)	stitch(es)

Body

Make 2ch.
Round 1: 6dc in second ch from hook.
Round 2: 2dc in each st. (*12 sts*).
Round 3: *1dc in next st, 2dc in next st; rep from * to end. (*18 sts*)
Round 4: *1dc in each of next 2 sts, 2dc in next st; rep from * to end. (*24 sts*)
Round 5: *1dc in each of next 3 sts, 2dc in next st; rep from * to end. (*30 sts*)
Round 6: *1dc in each of next 4 sts, 2dc in next st; rep from * to end. (*36 sts*)
Rounds 7–14: 1dc in each st.
Round 15: *1dc in each of next 4 sts, dc2tog; rep from * to end. (*30 sts*)
Round 16: *1dc in each of next 3 sts, dc2tog; rep from * to end. (*24 sts*)
Round 17: 1dc in each st.
Round 18: *1dc in each of next 2 sts, dc2tog; rep from * to end. (*18 sts*)
Round 19: 1dc in each st.
Round 20: *1dc in next st, dc2tog; rep from * to end. (*12 sts*)
Insert eyes and secure. Stuff body.
Rounds 21–22: 1dc in each st.
Round 23: *Miss 1 st, 1dc in next st; rep from * until opening is closed. Fasten off.

Ears

(make 2)
Make 2ch.
Round 1: 6dc in second st from hook.
Round 2: 2dc in each st. (*12 sts*)
Round 3: 1dc in each st.
Fasten off.

Tail

Make 20ch, turn, ss in each ch.
Fasten off.

Finishing

Sew ears on behind eyes.
Sew small triangle of white felt at end of muzzle for the nose.
Using white embroidery thread (floss) sew 3 long stitches each side of the nose for whiskers.
Pin and sew tail to body.

Baby Bouncers

These little crochet balls are perfect for tiny hands – lovely for babies to hold, throw or crawl after. They are also great for practising crocheting in the round, as well as using up smaller remnants of yarn. Make them using one colour or in stripes.

YARN AND MATERIALS

Any merino wool DK (light worsted) yarn similar to King Cole Merino Blend DK (100% wool; 104m/104yd per 50g/1¾oz ball)

- Small amount each in:
  Yellow
  Pink
  Lilac
  Pale green
  Pale blue
  Pale pink

Fibrefill stuffing

HOOKS AND EQUIPMENT

4mm (US size G/6) crochet hook

Stitch marker

Yarn needle

TENSION

Exact tension is not essential for this project, just adjust the hook size if necessary to achieve a firm fabric.

FINISHED MEASUREMENTS

Approx. 7.5cm (3in) in diameter

ABBREVIATIONS

beg	beginning
ch	chain
dc	double crochet
dc2tog	double crochet 2 stitches together.
ss	slip stitch
st(s)	stitch(es)

Bouncers

Place st marker at beg of each round.
Round 1: 2ch, 6dc into second ch from hook.
Round 2: 2dc in each st. (*12 sts*)
Round 3: *1dc in next st, 2dc; rep from * to end. (*18 sts*)
Round 4: *1dc in each of next 2 sts, 2dc; rep from * to end. (*24 sts*)
Round 5: *1dc in each of next 3 sts, 2dc; rep from * to end. (*30 sts*)
Rounds 6–10: 1dc in each st. (*30 sts*)
Round 11: *1dc in each of next 3 sts, dc2tog; rep from * to end. (*24 sts*)
Round 12: *1dc in each of next 2 sts, dc2tog; rep from * to end. (*18 sts*)
Round 13: *1dc in next st, dc2tog; rep from * to end. (*12 sts*)
Stuff ball.
Round 14: Dc2tog around until hole closes.
Fasten off.
Sew in ends.

Techniques

In this section, we explain how to master the simple crochet and finishing techniques that you need to make the projects in this book.

Holding the hook

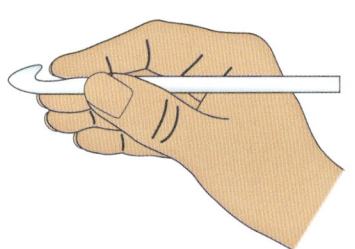

Pick up your hook as though you are picking up a pen or pencil. Keeping the hook held loosely between your fingers and thumb, turn your hand so that the palm is facing up and the hook is balanced in your hand and resting in the space between your index finger and your thumb.

You can also hold the hook like a knife – this may be easier if you are working with a large hook or with chunky yarn. Choose the method that you find most comfortable.

Holding the yarn

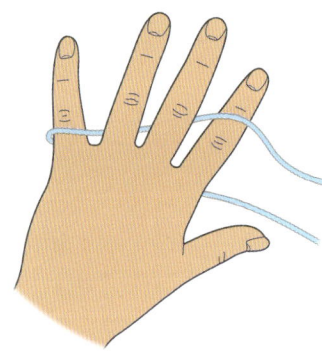 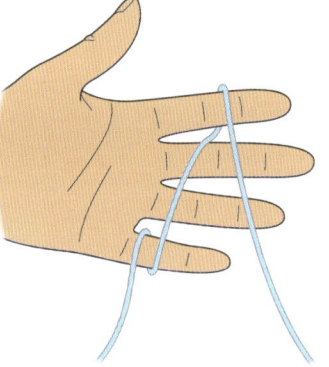

1 Pick up the yarn with your little finger in the opposite hand to your hook, with your palm facing upward and with the short end in front. Turn your hand to face downward, with the yarn on top of your index finger and under the other two fingers and wrapped right around the little finger, as shown above.

2 Turn your hand to face you, ready to hold the work in your middle finger and thumb. Keeping your index finger only at a slight curve, hold the work or the slip knot using the same hand, between your middle finger and your thumb and just below the crochet hook and loop/s on the hook.

Making a slip knot

The simplest way is to make a circle with the yarn, so that the loop is facing downward.

 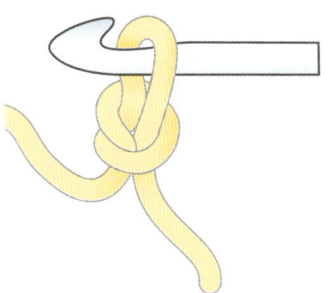

1 In one hand hold the circle at the top where the yarn crosses, and let the tail drop down at the back so that it falls across the centre of the loop. With your free hand or the tip of a crochet hook, pull a loop through the circle.

2 Put the hook into the loop and pull gently so that it forms a loose loop on the hook.

Yarn round hook (yrh)

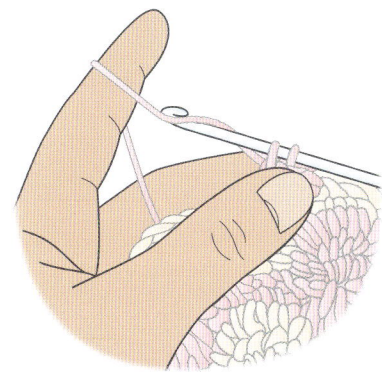

To create a stitch, catch the yarn from behind with the hook pointing upward. As you gently pull the yarn through the loop on the hook, turn the hook so it faces downward and slide the yarn through the loop. The loop on the hook should be kept loose enough for the hook to slide through easily.

Magic ring

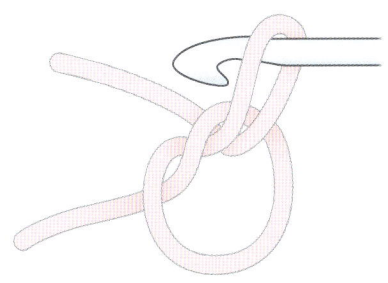

This is a useful starting technique if you do not want a visible hole in the centre of your round. Loop the yarn around your finger, insert the hook through the ring, yarn round hook, pull through the ring to make the first chain. Work the number of stitches required into the ring and then pull the end to tighten the centre ring and close the hole.

Chain (ch)

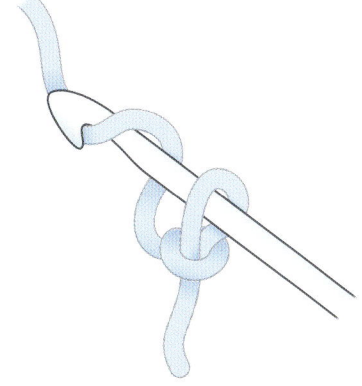

1 Using the hook, wrap the yarn round the hook ready to pull it through the loop on the hook.

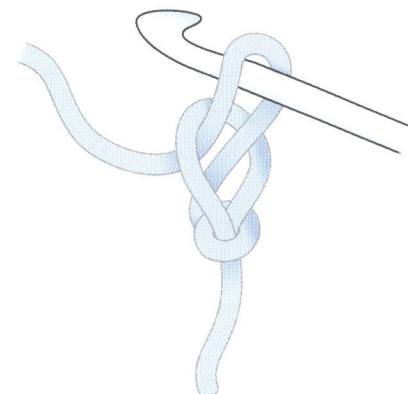

2 Pull through, creating a new loop on the hook. Continue in this way to create a chain of the required length.

Chain ring

If you are crocheting a round shape, one way of starting off is by crocheting a number of chains following the instructions in your pattern, and then joining them into a circle.

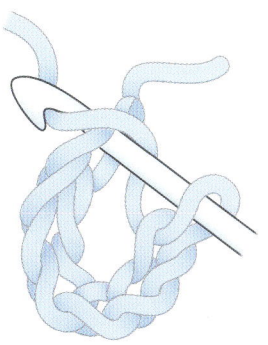

1 To join the chain into a circle, insert the crochet hook into the first chain that you made (not into the slip knot), yarn round hook.

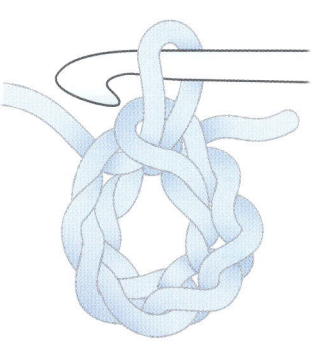

2 Pull the yarn through the chain and through the loop on your hook at the same time, thereby creating a slip stitch and forming a circle. You now have a chain ring ready to work stitches into as instructed in the pattern.

Chain space (ch sp)

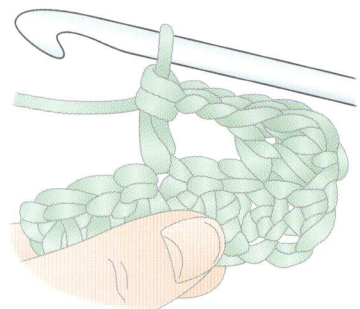

1 A chain space is the space that has been made under a chain in the previous round or row, and falls in between other stitches.

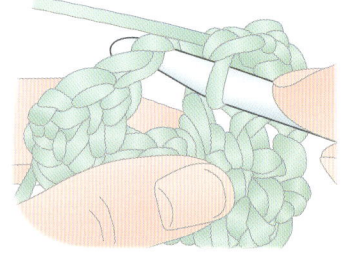

2 Stitches into a chain space are made directly into the hole created under the chain and not into the chain stitches themselves.

Slip stitch (sl st)

A slip stitch doesn't create any height and is often used as the last stitch to create a smooth and even round or row.

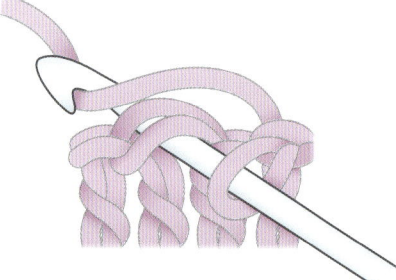

1 To make a slip stitch: first put the hook through the work, yarn round hook.

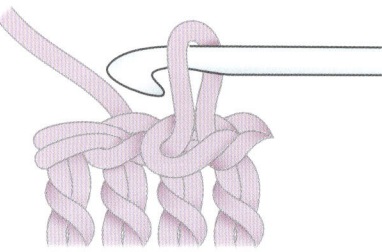

2 Pull the yarn through both the work and through the loop on the hook at the same time, so you will have 1 loop on the hook.

Making rounds

When working in rounds the work is not turned, so you are always working from one side. Depending on the pattern you are working, a 'round' can be square.

Start each round by making one or more chains to create a turning chain to the height you need for the stitch you are working:

Double crochet = 1 chain
Half treble crochet = 2 chains
Treble crochet = 3 chains
Double treble = 4 chains

Work the required stitches to complete the round. At the end of the round, slip stitch into the top of the chain to close the round.

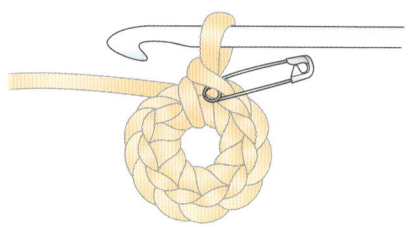

If you work in a spiral you do not need a turning chain. After completing the base ring, place a stitch marker in the first stitch and then continue to crochet around. When you have made a round and reached the point where the stitch marker is, work this stitch, take out the stitch marker from the previous round and put it back into the first stitch of the new round. A safety pin or piece of yarn in a contrasting colour makes a good stitch marker.

Making rows

When making straight rows you turn the work at the end of each row and make a turning chain to create the height you need for the stitch you are working with, as for making rounds.

Double crochet = 1 chain
Half treble crochet = 2 chains
Treble crochet = 3 chains
Double treble = 4 chains

Working into top of stitch

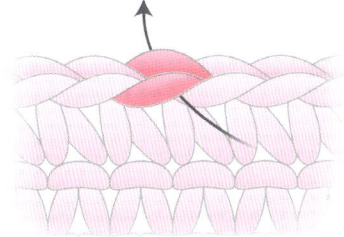

Unless otherwise directed, always insert the hook under both of the two loops on top of the stitch – this is the standard technique.

Working into front loop of stitch (FLO)

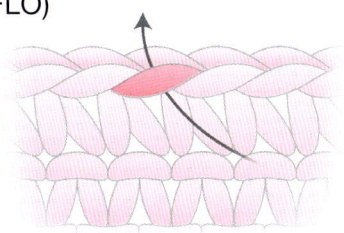

To work into the front loop of a stitch, pick up the front loop from underneath at the front of the work.

Working into back loop of stitch (BLO)

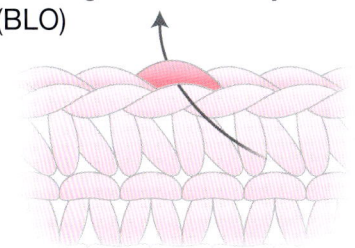

To work into the back loop of the stitch, insert the hook between the front and the back loop, picking up the back loop from the front of the work.

Working into both sides of a chain

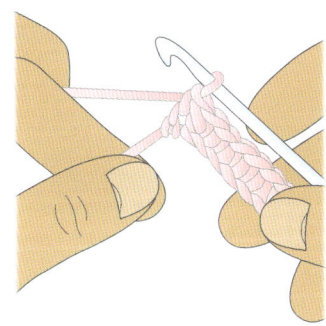

1 Make the required number of starting chains and work stitches as instructed in the pattern – you will be working a stitch into each chain and multiple stitches into the end chain.

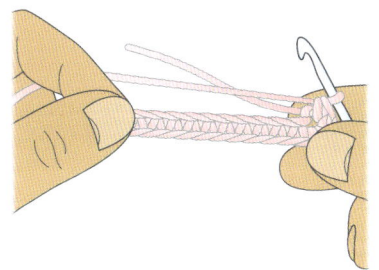

2 Turn the chain 180 degrees clockwise.

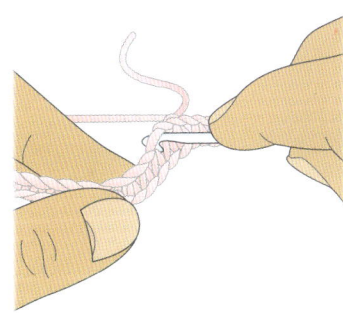

3 Work a stitch into each chain again along the other side of the chain, and multiple stitches into the end chain. Slip stitch to join for working in the round.

How to measure a tension (gauge) square

Using the hook and the yarn recommended in the pattern, make a number of chains to measure approximately 15cm (6in). Working in the stitch pattern given for the tension measurements, work enough rows to form a square. Fasten off.

Take a ruler, place it horizontally across the square and, using pins, mark a 10cm (4in) area. Repeat vertically to form a 10cm (4in) square on the fabric.

Count the number of stitches across, and the number of rows within the square, and compare against the tension given in the pattern.

If your numbers match the pattern then use this size hook and yarn for your project. If you have more stitches, then your tension is tighter than recommended and you need to use a larger hook. If you have fewer stitches, then your tension is looser and you will need a smaller hook.

Make tension squares using different size hooks until you have matched the tension in the pattern, and use this hook to make the project.

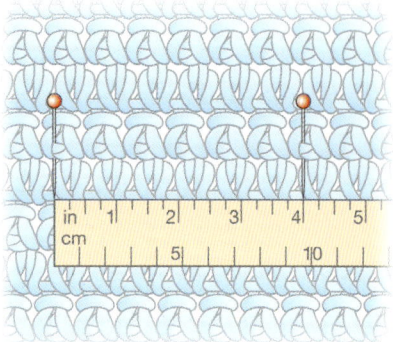

Double crochet (dc)

1 Insert the hook into your work, yarn round hook and pull the yarn through the work only (2 loops on the hook).

2 Yarn round hook again and pull through the 2 loops on the hook. (1 loop on the hook). One double crochet made.

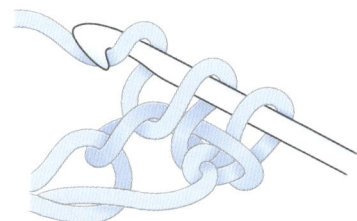

Half treble crochet (htr)

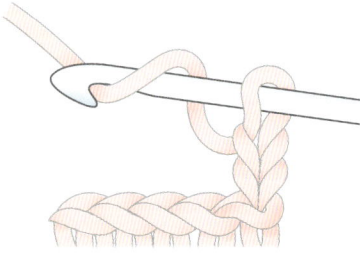

1 Before inserting the hook into the work, wrap the yarn round the hook and put the hook through the work with the yarn wrapped around.

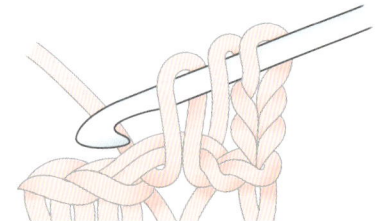

2 Yarn round hook again and pull through the first loop on the hook (3 loops on the hook).

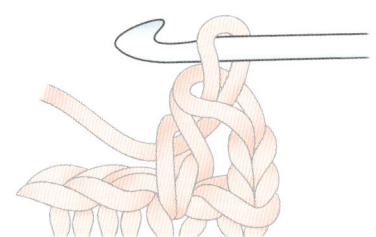

3 Yarn round hook and pull the yarn through all 3 loops (1 loop on the hook). One half treble crochet made.

Treble crochet (tr)

1 Before inserting the hook into the work, wrap the yarn round the hook. Put the hook through the work with the yarn wrapped around, yarn round hook again and pull through the first loop on the hook (3 loops on the hook).

2 Yarn round hook again, pull the yarn through the first 2 loops on the hook (2 loops on the hook).

3 Pull the yarn through 2 loops again (1 loop on the hook). One treble crochet made.

Double treble (dtr)

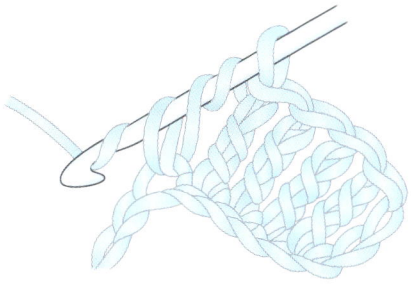

Yarn round hook twice, insert the hook into the stitch, yarn round hook, pull a loop through (4 loops on hook), yarn round hook, pull the yarn through 2 stitches (3 loops on hook), yarn round hook, pull a loop through the next 2 stitches (2 loops on hook), yarn round hook, pull a loop through the last 2 stitches (1 loop on the hook). One double treble made.

Triple treble (ttr)

Triple trebles are 'tall' stitches and are an extension on the basic treble stitch. They need a turning chain of 5 chains.

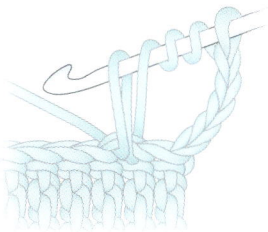 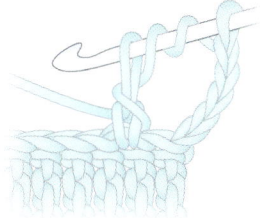

1 Yarn round hook 3 times, insert the hook into the stitch or space. Yarn round hook, pull the yarn through the work (5 loops on the hook).

2 Yarn round hook, pull the yarn through the first 2 loops on the hook (4 loops on the hook).

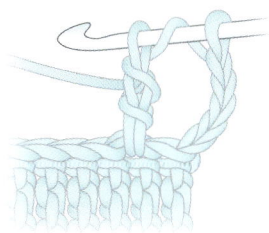 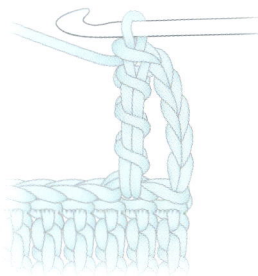

3 Yarn round hook, pull the yarn through the first 2 loops on the hook (3 loops on the hook).

4 Yarn round hook, pull the yarn through the first 2 loops on the hook (2 loops on hook). Yarn round hook, pull the yarn through the 2 loops on the hook (1 loop on the hook). One triple treble made.

Quadruple treble (qtr)

For qtr, begin by wrapping the yarn round the hook 4 times and then proceed in the same way as for triple treble (right) until you are left with 1 loop on the hook. One quadruple treble made.

Techniques **85**

Clusters

Clusters are groups of stitches, with each stitch only partly worked and then all joined at the end to form one stitch that creates a particular pattern and shape. They are most effective when made using a longer stitch such as a treble. Clusters can be made with any number of stitches and there can be variations in the exact way they are worked, so follow the special abbreviation instructions in each pattern.

TWO-TREBLE CLUSTER (2trCL)

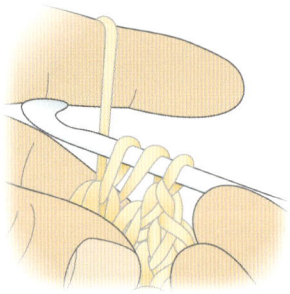

1 Yarn round hook, insert the hook in the stitch (or space). Yarn round hook, pull the yarn through the work (3 loops on the hook).

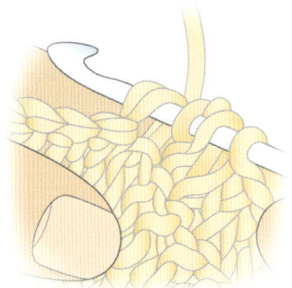

2 Yarn round hook, pull the yarn through 2 loops on the hook (2 loops on the hook). Yarn round hook, insert the hook in the same stitch (or space).

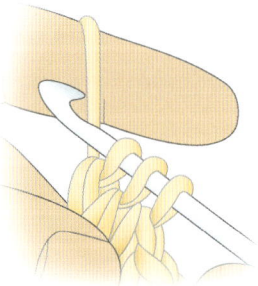

3 Yarn round hook, pull the yarn through the work (4 loops on the hook). Yarn round hook, pull the yarn through 2 loops on the hook (3 loops on the hook).

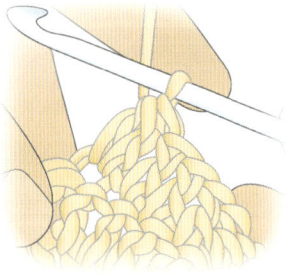

4 Yarn round hook, pull the yarn through all 3 loops on the hook (1 loop on hook). One two-treble cluster made.

THREE-TREBLE CLUSTER (3trCL)

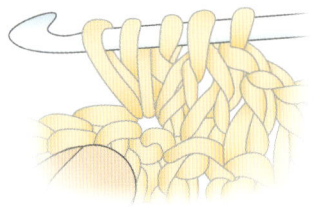

1 Work as 2trCL to end of step 3. Yarn round hook, insert the hook in the same stitch (or space), yarn round hook, pull the yarn through the work (5 loops on the hook).

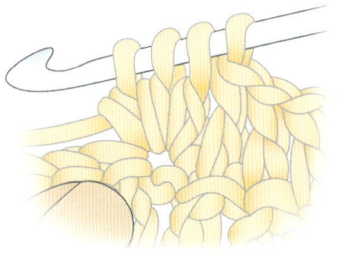

2 Yarn round hook, pull the yarn through 2 loops on the hook (4 loops on the hook).

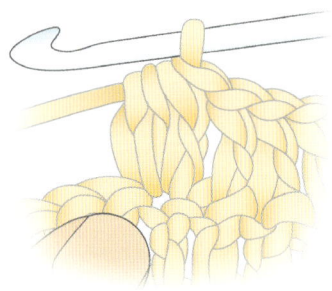

3 Yarn round hook, pull the yarn through all 4 loops on the hook (1 loop on the hook). One three-treble cluster made.

Picot

A picot is a little bobble texture that is often used to create little points along the outer edge of an edging. The illustrations show a three-chain picot, but they can be made with fewer or more chains.

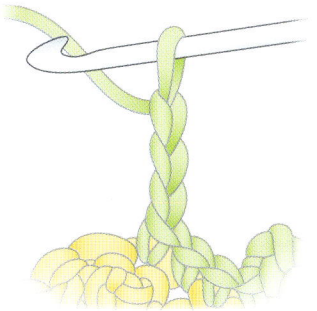

1 Work to the position of the picot, then make 3ch.

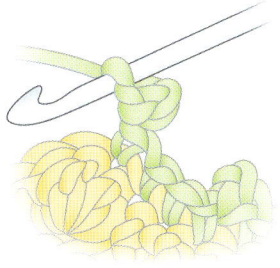

2 Ss in third ch from hook (1 picot made).

3 Continue making picots along the edge, spacing them with stitches as directed in the pattern.

Popcorn (PC)

This example shows a popcorn made with four treble stitches worked into a foundation chain, but a popcorn can be worked into any stitch or space and can be made up of any practical number or combination of stitches.

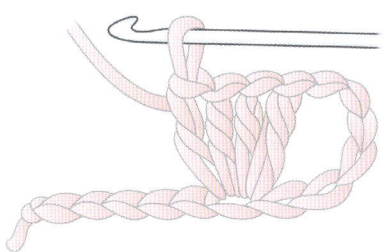

1 Inserting the hook in the same place each time, work 4 complete trebles.

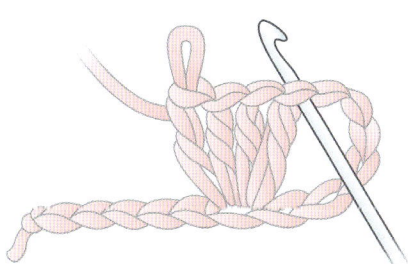

2 Slip the hook out of the last loop and insert it into the top of the first stitch.

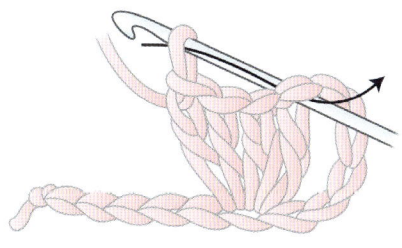

3 Then insert the hook into the loop of the last stitch again. Yarn round hook and pull it through as indicated.

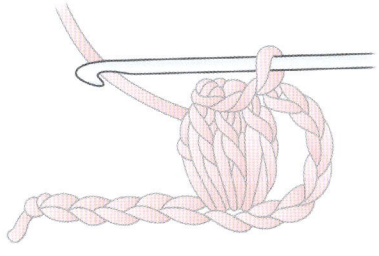

4 This makes one complete popcorn.

Increasing

Make two or three stitches into one stitch or space from the previous row. The illustration shows a treble crochet increase being made.

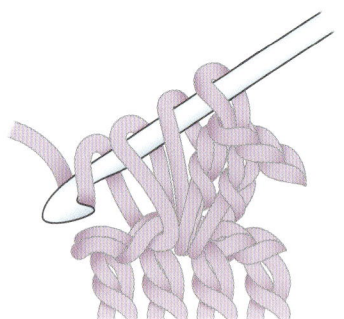

Decreasing

You can decrease by either missing the next stitch and continuing to crochet, or by crocheting two or more stitches together. The basic technique for crocheting stitches together is the same, no matter which stitch you are using.

DOUBLE CROCHET TWO STITCHES TOGETHER (dc2tog)

1 Insert the hook into your work, yarn round hook and pull the yarn through the work (2 loops on hook). Insert the hook in next stitch, yarn round hook and pull the yarn through.

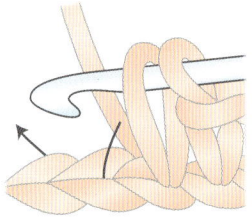

2 Yarn round hook again and pull through all 3 loops on the hook. You will then have 1 loop on the hook.

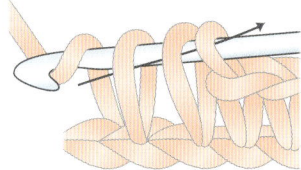

HALF TREBLE 2 STITCHES TOGETHER (htr2tog)

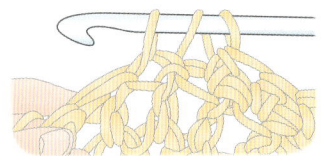
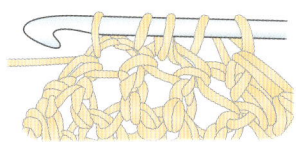

1 Yarn round hook, insert the hook into the next stitch, yarn round hook, draw the yarn through (3 loops on the hook).

2 Yarn round hook, insert the hook into the next stitch, yarn round hook, draw the yarn through the work (5 loops on the hook).

3 Yarn round hook, draw the yarn through all 5 loops on the hook (1 loop on hook).

TREBLE CROCHET TWO STITCHES TOGETHER (tr2tog)

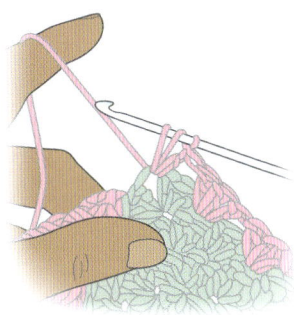 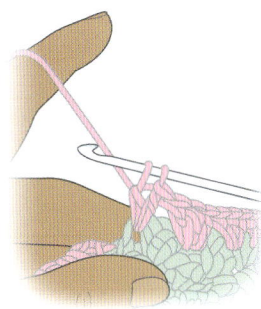 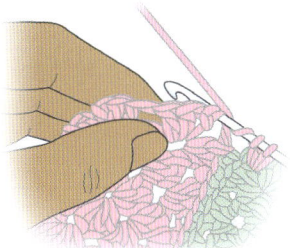

1 Yarn round hook, insert the hook into the next space, yarn round hook, pull the yarn through the work (3 loops on the hook).

2 Yarn round hook, pull the yarn through 2 loops on the hook (2 loops on the hook).

3 Yarn round hook, insert the hook into the next space.

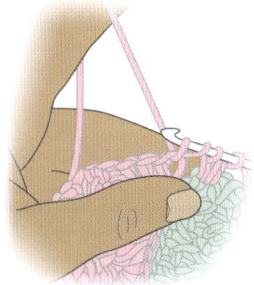 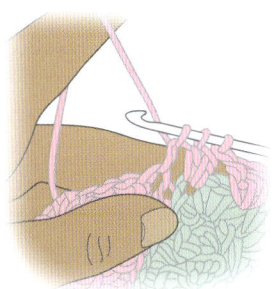 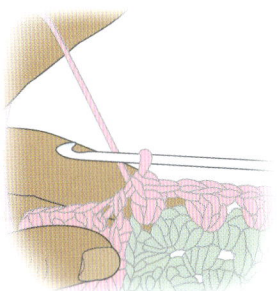

4 Yarn round hook, pull the yarn through the work (4 loops on the hook).

5 Yarn round hook, pull the yarn through 2 loops on the hook (3 loops on the hook).

6 Yarn round hook, pull the yarn through all 3 loops on the hook (1 loop on the hook).

TREBLE CROCHET 3 STITCHES TOGETHER (tr3tog)

Work a treble into each of the next three stitches as normal, but leave the last loop of each stitch on the hook (4 loops on the hook). Yarn round hook and pull the yarn through all the stitches on the hook to join them together (1 loop on the hook).

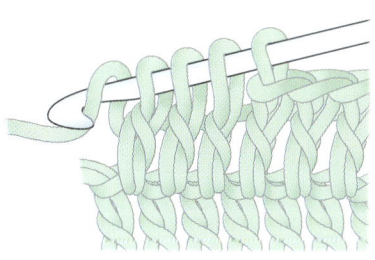

Joining yarn at the end of a row or round

You can use this technique when changing colour, or when joining in a new ball of yarn as one runs out.

1 Keep the loop of the old yarn on the hook. Drop the tail and catch a loop of the strand of the new yarn with the crochet hook.

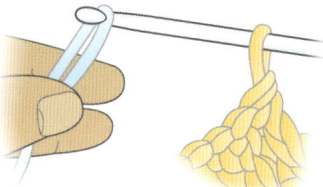

2 Draw the new yarn through the loop on the hook, keeping the old loop drawn tight and continue as instructed in the pattern.

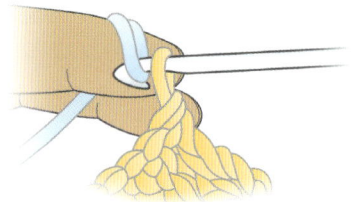

Joining in new yarn after fastening off

1 Fasten off the old colour (see page 91). Make a slip knot with the new colour (see page 80). Insert the hook into the stitch at the beginning of the next row, then through the slip knot.

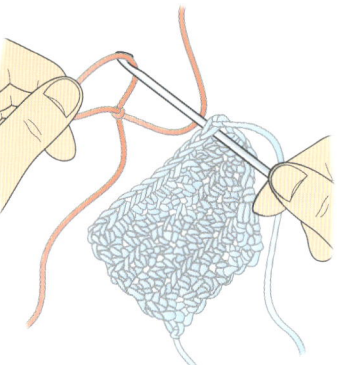

2 Draw the loop of the slip knot through to the front of the work. Carry on working using the new colour, following the instructions in the pattern.

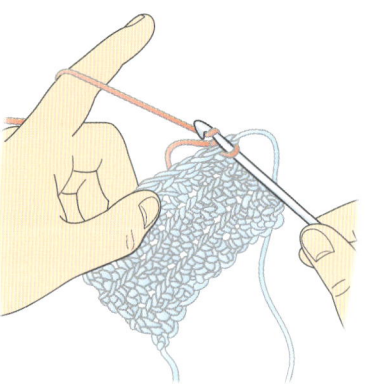

Joining yarn in the middle of a row or round

For a neat colour join in the middle of a row or round, use these methods.

JOINING A NEW COLOUR INTO DOUBLE CROCHET

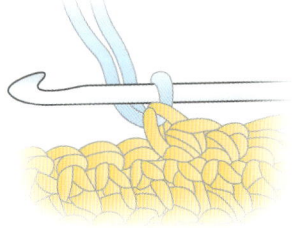 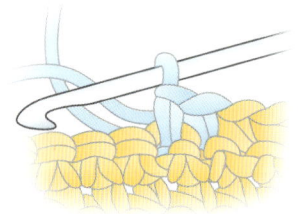

1 Make a double crochet stitch (see page 84), but do not draw the final loop through, so there are 2 loops on the hook. Drop the old yarn, catch the new yarn with the hook and draw it through both loops to complete the stitch and join in the new colour at the same time.

2 Continue to crochet with the new yarn. Cut the old yarn leaving a 15cm (6in) tail and weave the tail in (see opposite) after working a row, or once the work is complete.

JOINING A NEW COLOUR INTO TREBLE CROCHET

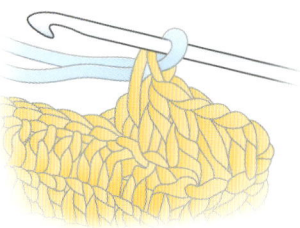 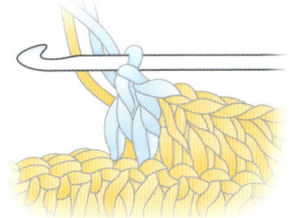

1 Make a treble crochet stitch (see page 85), but do not draw the final loop through, so there are 2 loops on the hook. Drop the old yarn, catch the new yarn with the hook and draw it through both loops to complete the stitch and join in the new colour at the same time.

2 Continue to crochet with the new yarn. Cut the old yarn leaving a 15cm (6in) tail and weave the tail in (see opposite) after working a row, opposite once the work is complete.

Enclosing a yarn tail

You may find that the yarn tail gets in the way as you work; you can enclose this into the stitches as you go by placing the tail at the back as you wrap the yarn. This also saves having to sew this tail end in later.

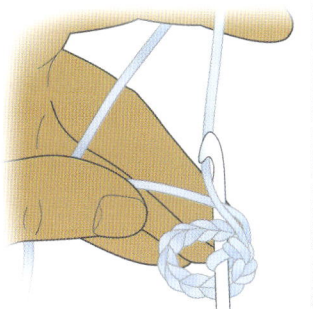

Fastening off

When you have finished crocheting, you need to fasten off the stitches to stop all your work unravelling.

Draw up the final loop of the last stitch to make it bigger. Cut the yarn, leaving a tail of approximately 10cm (4in) – unless a longer end is needed for sewing up. Pull the tail all the way through the loop and pull the loop up tightly.

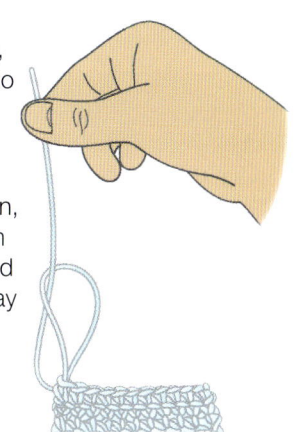

Weaving in yarn ends

It is important to weave in the tail ends of the yarn so that they are secure and your crochet won't unravel. Thread a yarn needle with the tail end of yarn. On the wrong side, take the needle through the crochet one stitch down on the edge, then take it through the stitches, working in a gentle zig-zag. Work through four or five stitches then return in the opposite direction. Remove the needle, pull the crochet gently to stretch it and trim the end.

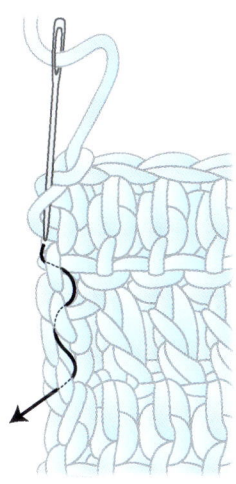

Blocking

Crochet can tend to curl, so to make flat pieces stay flat you may need to block them. Pin the piece out to the correct size and shape on an ironing board, then cover with a cloth and press or steam gently (depending on the type of yarn) and allow to dry completely before unpinning and removing from the board.

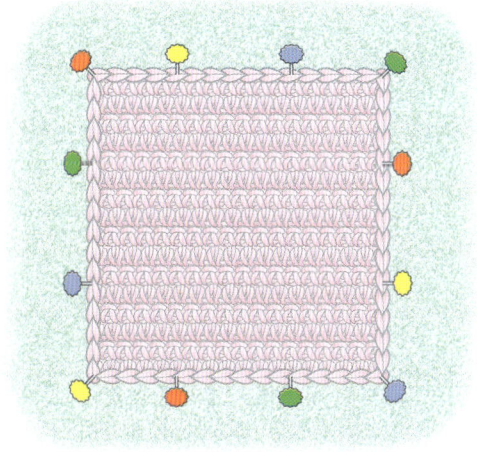

Techniques

Making an oversewn seam

An oversewn join gives a nice flat seam and is the simplest and most common joining technique.

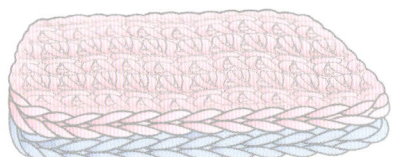
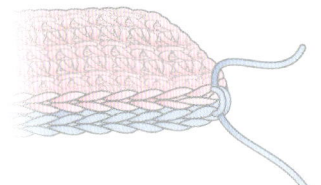
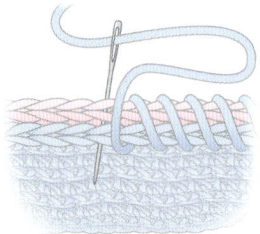

1 Thread a yarn needle with the yarn you're using in the project. Place the pieces to be joined with right sides together.

2 Insert the needle in one corner in the top loops of the stitches of both pieces and pull up the yarn, leaving a tail of about 5cm (2in). Go into the same place with the needle and pull up the yarn again; repeat two or three times to secure the yarn at the start of the seam.

3 Join the pieces together by taking the needle through the loops at the top of corresponding stitches on each piece to the end. Fasten off the yarn at the end, as in step 2.

Making a double crochet seam

With a double crochet seam you join two pieces together using a crochet hook and working a double crochet stitch through both pieces, instead of sewing them together with a tail of yarn and a yarn sewing needle. This makes a quick and strong seam and gives a slightly raised finish to the edging. For a less raised seam, follow the same basic technique, but work each stitch in slip stitch rather than double crochet.

1 Start by lining up the two pieces with wrong sides together. Insert the hook in the top 2 loops of the stitch of the first piece, then into the corresponding stitch on the second piece.

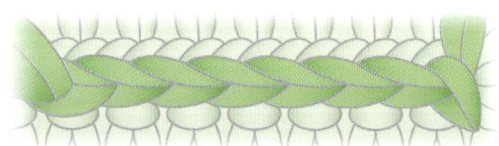

2 Complete the double crochet stitch as normal and continue on the next stitches as directed in the pattern. This gives a raised effect if the double crochet stitches are made on the right side of the work.

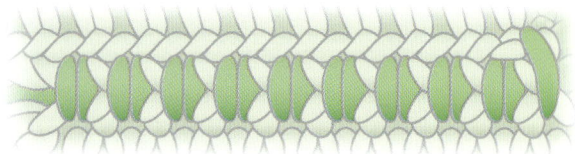

3 You can work with the wrong side of the work facing (with the pieces right side facing) if you don't want this effect and it still creates a good strong join.

French knots

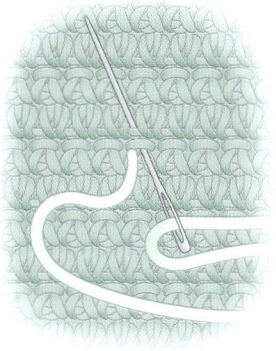

1 Thread the yarn into a yarn needle. Bring the yarn out at your starting point from the back of the work to the front and where you want the French knot to sit, leaving a tail of yarn at the back that you will sew in later. Pick up a couple of strands across the stitch on the front of the work close to the place the yarn has been pulled through.

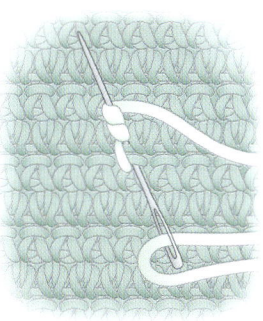

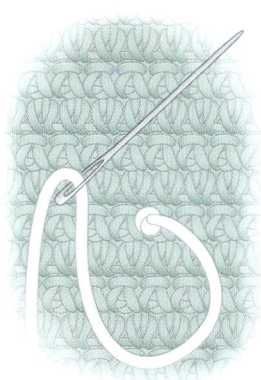

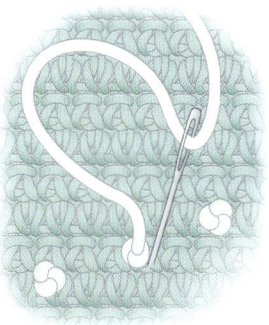

2 Wrap the yarn round the needle two or three times, pushing the wraps close to the crochet piece.

3 Take the needle in one hand and pull it through the wraps, holding the wraps in place near the crochet piece with the other hand. This will form a little knot close to the crochet piece.

4 Insert the needle (from the right side) very close to the knot and push the needle through to the wrong side (French knot made).

Adding safety eyes

Safety eyes are a great choice to add character to your toys, but make sure they are firmly fixed in place. If the toy is for a very young child, it is probably better to embroider the eyes after the toy is finished.

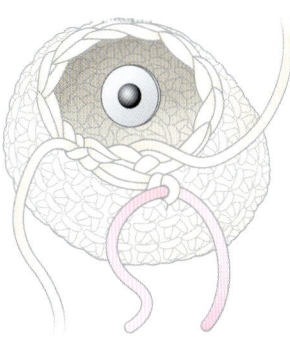

1 Insert the safety eyes in place on the face from the right side.

2 Make sure they are completely level and sitting on the same row before you secure the safety catches at the back. The flat piece of the safety catch is pushed towards the crochet piece from the inside.

Techniques **93**

TEMPLATE

PICKLE THE PUPPY'S SCARF

pages 64–66

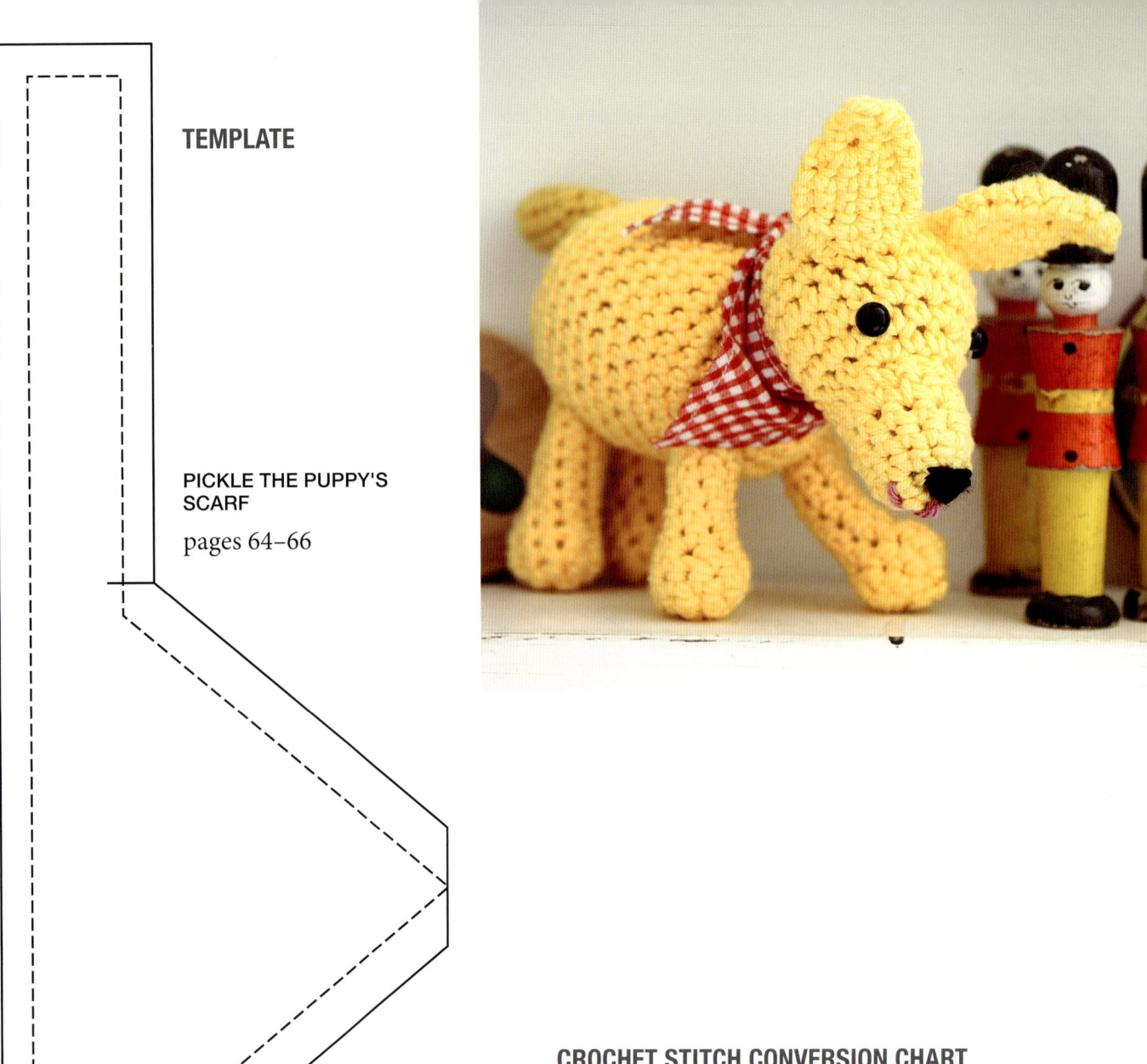

CROCHET STITCH CONVERSION CHART

Crochet stitches are worked in the same way in both the UK and the USA, but the stitch names are not the same and identical names are used for different stitches. Below is a list of the UK terms used in this book, and the equivalent US terms.

UK TERM	US TERM
double crochet (dc)	single crochet (sc)
half treble (htr)	half double crochet (hdc)
treble (tr)	double crochet (dc)
double treble (dtr)	treble (tr)
triple treble (ttr)	double treble (dtr)
quadruple treble (qtr)	triple treble (ttr)
tension	gauge
yarn round hook (yrh)	yarn over hook (yoh)

Abbreviations

alt	alternat(e)ing
approx.	approximately
beg	beginning
BLO	back loop only
cm	centimetre(s)
cont	continu(e)ing
ch	chain
dc	double crochet
dc2tog	double crochet 2 stitches together
dec	decreas(e)ing
dtr	double treble
FLO	front loop only
foll	follow(s)ing
g	gram(mes)
htr	half treble
in	inch(es)
inc	increas(e)ing
m	metre(s)
mm	millimetre(s)
oz	ounce(s)
PM	place marker
prev	previous
qtr	quadruple treble
rem	remaining
rep	repeat
RS	right side
sl st	slip stitch
st(s)	stitch(es)
tog	together
tr	treble
ttr	triple treble
yd	yard(s)
WS	wrong side
yrh	yarn round hook
[ ]	work section between square brackets number of times stated
*	asterisk indicates beginning of repeated section of pattern

Suppliers

The projects in this book are great for using up leftover yarn in your craft supply.

If you wish to accurately substitute a different yarn for the one recommended in the pattern, try the Yarnsub website for suggestions: www.yarnsub.com

I also recommend exploring your local yarn stores to support small business owners and see what treasures you might find.

UK

LoveCrafts
www.lovecrafts.com

Wool
Store in Bath
Tel: +44 (0)1225 469144
www.woolbath.co.uk

VV Rouleaux
Stores in London and Bath
Tel: +44 (0)1225 618600
www.vvrouleaux.com

Laughing Hens
Tel: +44 (0)1829 740903
www.laughinghens.com

John Lewis
Store locations on website
www.johnlewis.com

Hobbycraft
www.hobbycraft.co.uk

USA

Knitting Fever Inc.
www.knittingfever.com

WEBS
www.yarn.com

Michaels
www.michaels.com

AUSTRALIA

Sunspun
Store in Canterbury, Victoria
Tel: +61 (0)3 9830 1609
www.sunspun.com.au

YARN COMPANIES

Rowan Yarns
www.knitrowan.com

Debbie Bliss
www.debbieblissonline.com

King Cole
www.kingcole.com

Hoooked
www.hoookedyarn.com

Lana Grossa
www.lana-grossa.de/en

Sirdar (Hayfield)
www.sirdar.com

index

abbreviations 95
animals
   Billy the Bear 73–75
   Melody the Kitten 67–69
   Pickle the Puppy 64–66
   sugar mice 76–77

babies
   baby pompon hat 36–37
   beanie hat 28–29
   lilac bootees 30–32
   star stitch bootees 33–35
baby bouncers 78
beanie hat 28–29
Billy the Bear 73–75
blanket, Ophelia 42–43
blocking work 91
bobble cafetière cosy 15–16
bootees
   lilac bootees 30–32
   star stitch bootees 33–35
brooch, flower 58–59
buggy blanket 42–43
bunny egg cosies 11
bunting 51–53
butterfly and blossom key ring 60–61

cafetière cosy 15–16
chains 81
   chain ring 81
   chain space 82
   working into both sides of a chain 83
chickens coat hanger 40–41
clusters 86
coaster, vintage-style 23–25
coat hangers, nursery 38–41
conversion chart 94
cosies
   bobble cafetière cosy 15–16
   bunny egg cosies 11
   crochet hook cosy 57
   jam jar tea light cosies 49–50
   mug cosies 12–13
   striped phone cosy 46–47
cushion cover, stripy 17–19

decreasing stitches 88–89
double crochet 84
   decreasing 88
   double crochet seams 92
double treble 85

edgings, picot 86
egg cosies, bunny 11
eyes, safety 93

fastening off 91
flags, bunting 52–53
flowers
   bunting 53
   butterfly and blossom key ring 60–61
   flower brooch 58–59
   nursery coat hangers 41
French knots 93

gauge (tension) squares 84

half treble crochet 84
   decreasing 88
hats
   baby pompon hat 36–37
   beanie hat 28–29
holding hooks 80
holding yarn 80
hooks
   crochet hook cosy 57
   holding 80

increasing stitches 88

jam jar tea light cosies 49–50
joining yarn 90–91

key ring, butterfly and blossom 60–61
kittens 67–69
knots
   French knots 93
   slip knots 80

leaves, nursery coat hangers 38–41
lilac bootees 30–32

magic ring 81
mats 20–22
measuring tension (gauge) squares 84
Melody the Kitten 67–69
mice 76–77
mug cosies 12–13

nursery coat hangers 38–41

Ophelia buggy blanket 42–43
oversewn seams 92

phone cosy, striped 46–47
Pickle the Puppy 64–66
picot 86
pin cushions 54–55
placemats 20–22
pompom hat 36–37
popcorn 86
pressing work 91

puppies 64–66

quadruple treble 85

round shapes 81
rounds, working in 82
rows, making 82

safety eyes 93
seams
   double crochet seams 92
   oversewn seams 92
slip knots 80
slip stitch 82
Sparkles the Snowman 70–72
star stitch bootees 33–35
stitches 84–85
   clusters 86
   decreasing 88–89
   increasing 88
   slip stitch 82
   working into 83
striped phone cosy 46–47
stripy cushion cover 17–19
sugar mice 76–77

tea light cosies 49–50
techniques 80–93
tension (gauge) squares 84
three-treble cluster 86
toys 63–79
   baby bouncers 78
   Billy the Bear 73–75
   Melody the Kitten 67–69
   Pickle the Puppy 64–66
   Sparkles the Snowman 70–72
   sugar mice 76–77
treble crochet 85
   decreasing 89
triple treble 85
two-treble cluster 86

vintage-style vase coaster 23–25

watermelon coat hanger 40–41
weaving in yarn ends 91

yarn
   enclosing tails 91
   fastening off 91
      holding 80
   joining 90–91
   substituting one yarn for another 7, 95
   weaving in ends 91
   yarn round hook 81